COUNSELING
THE   DYING

HARPER'S MINISTERS PAPERBACK LIBRARY

COUNSELING
THE   DYING

Margaretta K. Bowers
Edgar N. Jackson
James A. Knight
Lawrence LeShan

WITHDRAW

1817

HARPER & ROW, PUBLISHERS, San Francisco
Cambridge, Hagerstown, New York, Philadelphia
London, Mexico City, São Paulo, Sydney

COUNSELING THE DYING. Copyright © 1964 by Thomas Nelson & Sons. Introduction to the Paperback Edition copyright © 1981 by Edgar N. Jackson. All rights reserved. Printed in the United States of America. No part of this book may be used or reproduced in any manner whatsoever without written permission except in the case of brief quotations embodied in critical articles and reviews. For further information address Harper & Row, Publishers, Inc., 10 East 53rd Street, New York, NY 10022. Published simultaneously in Canada by Fitzhenry & Whiteside, Limited, Toronto.

First Harper & Row paperback edition published in 1981.

Library of Congress Cataloging in Publication Data
Main entry under title:

Counseling the dying.
   (Harper's ministers paperback library)
   Bibliography: p. 173.
    1. Death—Psychological aspects. 2. Counseling. 3. Terminal care—Psychological aspects. I. Bowers, Margaretta K. II. Series.
BF789.D4C68   1981   155.9'37   80-8903
                                            AACR2

ISBN 0-06-061020-4

81 82 83 84 85 10 9 8 7 6 5 4 3 2 1

CONTENTS

INTRODUCTION TO THE
PAPERBACK EDITION

I am glad for the chance to say a word of welcome for this paperback edition of a book that has been around in more expensive editions for nearly two decades. Before the plethora of books exploring the human experience of death and dying had become available, this book was serving a useful purpose. In fact, the *Journal of Pastoral Care* asserted, "It has the characteristics of a classic. . . . It creates a reflective mood which carries the readers into the context of a deathbed experience without being sentimental or melodramatic. . . . It is written in a way that will always be relevant, informative and inspirational."

I am also pleased with the prospects for this new edition for two other reasons: the verification of its basic thesis by recent developments in the care of the catastrophically ill and the new validity accorded its assumptions by developments in medical humanities, the hospice movement, and the active interest in holistic medicine.

When a book pioneers in a relatively new field of interest, it is fortunate when the blending of many disciplines makes it possible for broad perspectives to be brought into play. If we examine the roles of the coauthors of this book, we find an internist, a clinical psychologist, a psychoanalyst, a professor of psychiatry, a crisis psychologist, a research psychologist, a gynecologist-obstetrician, two ordained clergymen, a hospital chaplain, a registered nurse, a general practitioner, a seminary professor, and four parents, each with a special interst and skill in caring for seriously ill persons. Certainly these varied perspectives have given to our book a depth that would not have been achieved by the most discerning lone person.

Our basic assumption was that dying persons are no less persons because they are nearing the end of their earthly pilgrimage. With that in mind, we tried to understand all of the resources available for communication and relationship with the dying. We sought to nurture the human dimension as long as possible. We discovered ways of sustaining life that were not easily discernible to those who sought to meet only the diminishing physical needs. In fact, we came to the conclusion that many people die because they are not given the opportunity to respond within the bounds of their full humanity.

Our indebtedness to hospice idea and to its mentor, Cecily Saunders, M.D., is considerable. Those of use who went to London to explore her treatment methods were impressed by the way she brought together the best of medical insight, social-work skills, religious awareness, and warm human interest. Her combination of approaches bore specific results in the wiser management of anxiety and the reduction of pain. The open and therapeutic use of communication changed the treatment center from a place where anxiety was created and nurtured to a place where sharing of thought, feeling, and experience made it possible for apprehension to be reduced, pain relieved, and specific therapeutic results observed.

Perhaps without realizing the significance of what we were doing, we anticipated the awareness of major crises in health perceptions and started a process of reexamination. We concluded that in at least four significant areas, a larger perception of the person was essential to wise health care.

First, there was a need to move beyond mechanistic perceptions of physical processes. While some muscular and skeletal functions quite obviously have mechanical processes at work, it is impossible to extrapolate that all of life is based on mechanical priciples. We cannot talk to machines, but we can talk to people, and they can talk back. A larger principle is at work; reductionist approaches are not only inadequate, they can be dangerous. Our assumption that life is more than mechanics is increasingly justified.

Second, our approach to chemistry opens a door to valued therapeutic intervention. Body chemistry and the function of the glandular system as the complicted factory for the body's chemicals must be seen in a larger context. Modification of the chemistry of the body by injesting and injecting chemicals may well be supplemented by modification of the emotional climate so that the body's own chemical resources are brought into more active cooperation with other forms of intervention. Immunotherapy in the past decade has become aware of internal processes that can supplement externally supplied medicines; our preview of this form of patient care has been verified.

Third, the expansion of electronic medicine—the computerization and electronic diagnostic devices that have changed the approach of medicine during the past decade or two—may further impersonalize the patient. While important benefits have been realized in some aspects of patient care through improved technology, a preoccupation with gadgetry can become yet another barrier between the ailing person and those who provide care at a time when the human dimension most needs to be empahasized.

Fourth, there must be an adequate philosophical base for understanding a patient's needs. Too often, efforts have been made to create a philosophy out of an accumulation of clinical observations. This always seems to result in an inadequate conception of what a human being is. Our effort to more sharply define the nature of a human being and the cosmological framework within which the human functions helped to produce a more adequate framework for the care of the patient confronting death. The implications of this philosophical stance might be of use in understanding patients in all of their treatment. This perception has been supported by much that is being done in a holistic approach to the patient and patient care.

While some conditions in medical care may have revealed technical and philosophical limitations, there have certainly been some positive developments that open the way for greater understanding of and response to the patient needs of the person who is dying.

Instead of asking, "What is the matter with this patient?" and, "What can we do to relive these symptoms?" psychosomatic research is now increasingly asking, "What is this organic behavior we call disease trying to tell us about the needs of this patient?" When illness is seen as a body metaphor trying to communicate patient needs, the role of the interpreter takes on a different meaning. Then the behavior of the dying patient may speak of despair and confusion more than of organic insufficiency, and the treatment may be vastly different.

Dramatic brain research in the last decade has changed our understanding of the nature and function of pain. In a relatively stress-free environment, production of molecules in the pineal gland that reduce pain may be encouraged and the treatment plan for a dying patient thus modified. Also, relaxation—through hearing of music, for example—may stimulate the flow of material across the corpus callosum so that damaged hemispheric conditions can be more effectively modified and communication restored. In that way, some of the life-impairing isolation of the stroke victim may be modified and the will to live restored.

The holistic approach so extensively used by Hospice, Inc., has verified our earlier awareness of the importance of the granting of full humanity to the desperately ill and dying patient. Isolation and abandonment impair life processes just as the enrichment of communication and relationship make life more worth living. Experience with holistic approaches tends to verify our feeling that many patients die who do not need to die, because life has needlessly become empty and meaningless. Life is social as well as physical; one aspect supports the other.

Our emphasis on the importance of attitudes has been verified by an accumulation of experience as reflected in James Lynch's studies in the intensive care, coronary care, and trauma units at the University Hospital in Baltimore. Other research among the emotionally injured also tends to confirm the observation that the will to live and the will to die have statistically significant manifestations among critically ill patients. It is also possible to show statistically that fear of death sometimes prolongs painful living when permission to die might provide blessed release from life that has lost significant relationship.

These various factors may indicate that we are ready for a quantum leap in understanding the needs of dying patients and for the possibility of more adequate care for those needs. We may gain new concepts of the health of the dying. In a four-volume guide to health, the index moves blithely from harelip to hepatitis; there is no question of health as a viable possibility for life. Perhaps our studies of the possibility of healthful dying could restore more healthful attitudes toward all of living.

Philosophically, our approach needs to be expanded and enriched by study and experience. When we get a clearer image of a human being, an image that incorporates all human dimensions, it will inevitably affect our care of the dying. Life will be experienced not so much in terms of quantity as of quality. We will sense the cosmic quality of every human soul and encourage its growth even through the events of dying. Cosmologically, we will be aware of the mysterious dimension of life and its energies and will learn ways of nurturing those energies as long as life endures. In this interplay of the personal and cosmic, we will undoubtedly discover perspectives on the experience of those who die that will enrich our understanding of our own living. That enriched understanding will enable us to achieve new levels of sensitivity in the care of the dying. Personhood will be enhanced to the end of the biological journey with the feeling that other, nonbiological aspects of being will continue to be verified in their own way.

New professional skills related to the care of the dying will develop as the philosophical perceptions grow. These professional skills will use biomedical insight but will add tender love and care and compassion of touch so that persons will complete their pilgrimage in this life with a sure knowledge of their own value and others' affectionate regard.

New goals in patient care will develop as the special ministry to those who are dying comes to be seen as an opportunity to verify the value of life. The Nazi experience showed us that when life is degraded anywhere, it is degraded everywhere. Conversely, when life is enhanced anywhere, all humanity benefits.

Much is happening in our world to improve the lot of the dying. Much more needs to be done. This is one time we are glad to have started something we couldn't finish. The phenomena surrounding dying form a large stage. We may be approaching a dramatic breakthrough in understanding that will set the stage for a far more creative approach to the needs of counseling the dying, for we will know more clearly that their needs are really our needs. In our search for a large enough philosophy of life and death, we are really seeking a significance for our own living and our own practice of the humanitarian skills that enrich all of life. Let us keep on at the task.

Edgar N. Jackson
Corinth, Vermont

INTRODUCTION TO THE FIRST EDITION

At the beginning of this inquiry it is only reasonable that we set our objectives and outline the approach to our goals.

Dying is an important event in the life history of the individual. Dying is a private affair. Each person must do his own dying. Birth is a social act, for no one is ever born alone. Dying is different. The end of life comes to each person as an intensely personal experience.

We have explored the literature on this subject and find that there is very little in the English language that would be primarily useful to the counselor. There are numerous books about the act of birth that explore the psychological and social meaning of the event. Careful study has been given to the "birth trauma." Treatises have compared the effect of "easy" and "difficult" birth on the personality of each individual born. But we find nothing comparable in literature to contrast "easy" and "difficult" dying.

We agree at the beginning that all dying is not the same. The prison chaplain counsels the man who is about to be executed and who knows the time, the place, and the reasons for his death. The split second accident on the highway takes life so quickly that the dying person does not know what has happened. The elderly person in a nursing home watches the inexorable advance of death and feels the ebbing of his own life's energy. The patient ill with cancer stands near the

1

center of an emotional battlefield as the forces of life and death contend. The despairing person, overwhelmed by the injuries of life and unable to face the future, plans his own death and performs the act of self-execution. The soldier at the front watches his comrades being killed and is aware of the possibility of his own death. The quiet soul who has lived a long and useful life and, worn with the years and deep fatigue, lies down to welcome a healthful death, shares a different need but a common event.

We believe that death is a far more important event in the psychological history of the individual than is usually faced. Herman Feifel shows that a primary subconscious concern of the person over fifty, as revealed through projective testing, is preoccupation with his own death. The existential philosophers have made us aware of the contrast between meaningless life and meaningful death. For some persons there is the need to die with meaning and dignity even though life may have been sordid and uncreative. As with the swan and its mythical final song and the animal that is reputed to return to its "dying place" there is apparently an innate mystical meaning in the terminal event of life.

If the event of death is important to the individual, the process of preparation for it is also not to be treated as trivial. The lifelong process of increasing the sources of energy is contending with an inexorable process of the breaking down of energy. Organically speaking, the physical being is in the process of dying from the time of conception. The importance of this fact for the subtle inner movement of thought and feeling cannot be ignored. Much basic anxiety may be related to this fact, and the primary function of most religions appears to be to ameliorate the emotional pain of contemplating death by making it an ultimately acceptable event.

Seen from the point of view of those who assume professionally a relationship to persons who are in the final stages of life, or the terminal phases of the process of dying, there are special attitudes and assumptions that have to be considered. The need of the counselor subtly conditions the nature of the counseling relationship. Since the basic assumptions of the professional persons differ, it is important for shared insight and experience to be brought into focus.

We who are engaging in this inquiry share a common interest but a widely varied experience. Margaretta Bowers is a practicing psychoanalyst who was for years a general practitioner working intensively in the field of obstetrics and gynecology. Prior to that she received training in the nursing profession. James A. Knight is a professor of psychiatry on the staff of a medical school and of a theological seminary. He served as a chaplain on a U.S. naval hospital ship during World War II. Lawrence LeShan is a clinical psychologist who for fourteen years has been doing research and therapy with cancer patients as a staff member of a hospital in New York City. Edgar N. Jackson has been in the pastoral ministry for thirty years and has nine years of clinical experience in hospitals and clinics. During World War II he served as a chaplain in the Army Air Force. We have spent thousands of hours with persons who were in the varied stages of terminal illness. We share our thoughts, feelings, and professional insight in the hope that it may make it possible for others to counsel more wisely and minister more effectively to persons whose needs are both unique and universal, intensely personal and socially significant.

However, in the act of sharing our experience with each other we have become aware of the unconscious conditioning our professional roles have created for us. We have been aware of the problems of communication and the hazards of language even when our disposition has been to under-

3

stand and share. What we hope will be useful to others has been first of all useful to us, for we have enriched our lives by the intensive sharing of thought and feeling on this subject of inquiry. In doing this we have been aware of the directions our professional training has set for us. The physician is trained to think of death as his enemy and to fight death as the way of preserving life. His idea of death is primarily organic and biological. The clinical psychologist, as well as the psychiatrist, is trained to understand the meaning of behavior, and he is concerned about what is going on deep within the mind and emotion of the patient. He is professionally neutral about death in general, but deeply concerned about the meaning of death to the individual with whom he counsels. The pastor is committed to the inevitability of physical death, but is concerned that his counselee find a meaning in life so rich in value that he will not be overwhelmed by the biologic incident related to mortality. These varied points of view tend to season the role and relationship of the counselor. When the background training of the physician and the pastor is enriched by psychological insight, and the clinical psychologist is enmeshed in the routine and philosophy of the hospital, some interesting and fruitful cross-fertilizations take place. It is this synthesis which has emerged for us and which we are trying to present in this book.

ONE

PRESUPPOSITIONS
IN COUNSELING THE DYING

The dying patient presents special opportunities and hazards to the counselor. To avoid an effective relationship because of fear and anxiety destroys the opportunity to talk with and feel the special needs of the patient. On the other hand, to overidentify with the patient can create conditions of mind and emotion that threaten the counselor. It has been observed clinically that such overidentification may actually produce severe psychic disturbances.

Part of the difficulty in establishing a healthy communication with the dying patient is the conspiracy of silence surrounding the subject of death. We have built social taboos around our mortality. The Victorian taboo about sex has been overcome in recent decades through the influence of Freud and Havelock Ellis, and many of the suppressed anxieties about sexuality can now be brought into the open. The importance of sex for life can be explored in an air not only of tolerance but of valid acceptance. With the exception of Jung's work, this is not yet the case with death.

While death is experienced all about us, we have built up walls against the healthful discussion of its meanings for persons and society. We show our anxiety by the devices we employ to wall the subject off from the therapeutic discussion. We make light of death by making it seem trivial and unimportant. We create the dramatic episodes on the

5

stage and in the films that make it possible for the same persons to die again and again as if it were possible to experience death with impunity. We watch the same person being killed week after week on television as if there were nothing final about it. We act as if our avoidance of discussion were an act of control of the circumstance. Such avoidance, far from removing the problem, only compounds the difficulty in facing it, and affirms the degree of our anxiety about it.

The dying patient, living in this unreal and prohibited atmosphere, is caught in the social restraint that makes his need greater at the same time that the opportunity to satisfy it is made increasingly difficult. This separates him from the normal communications of family and community by a conspiracy of silence and he is more completely alone when he most needs human contacts.

This mood of separation is often justified as an act of consideration and courage when actually it is a culturally imposed expression of anxiety. Professional persons are not immune from its effects.

This places a special responsibility on professionals, for in our culture most persons die in surroundings isolated from the general community, in hospitals, whereas a century ago most persons died at home. The hospital is the special domain of doctors and nurses, and if they are not prepared to counsel with the dying, the separation of the person from community support is acute. Yet too often those who are trained to preserve life are not as adequately prepared to minister to the special emotional needs of the dying.

Nurses are often closest to the patient during the period preceding death and would normally be the ones with whom effective communication might take place. But even here the prevailing need of our culture is subtly at work to isolate the patient. Dr. LeShan reports a telling piece of observation he set up in a large general hospital in New York. He classified the patients on one floor according to their nearness to death. Then he took his place, stop watch in hand, at the visitors' alcove at the end of the corridor where he could observe the light over the door of each room. He timed the interval between the appearance of the light over the door and the time the nurse entered the room of the patient. For several days he kept track of the time intervals, and correlated these with the condition of the patient. He found that the nurses consistently hurried to the rooms of the patients who were less near death, and as consistently dragged their feet in response to the summons of those who were at death's door. After completing his observations he asked the nurses why they responded less readily to the needs of those who were near death than they did to other patients in their care. They were surprised and shocked at the charge and at first denied it vigorously. Then, when the facts were laid before them, they had no explanation, for they had not been conscious of what they were doing. Their behavior had evidently been an unconscious expression of their aversion to death which had interfered with their care of their patients.

If this is a clue, it appears that actually the dying patient is unconsciously separated from the very communications that could undergird him emotionally and sustain him *in extremis*. Yet persons keep on dying and the encounter of the living and the dying goes on. Does it produce insights that can be useful for the counselor?

The values that are prevalent in any culture tend to project themselves into the personal events in the lives of its members, even the event of dying. The quest for status shows itself in attitudes toward disease and dying. The cancer patient is less apt to talk about his condition because his disease is not socially acceptable, while the heart patient is more inclined to talk about his ailment because it is considered a badge of honor, a clean and acceptable physical condition.

Eissler in his book, *The Psychiatrist and the Dying Patient*,[1] does a pioneering task in trying to define the therapist's role with the person facing death. His conclusion is that one tries to give meaning to death in accord with the person's meaning for life, so that the act of dying is not separated from life but is rather a continuation of the mood and manner of living.

Dr. Robert N. Butler,[2] of Washington, D.C., has observed that with dying persons there is often toward the end of life a strenuous effort both on conscious and unconscious levels to bring order and meaning into life, as if to end things in a tidy way. This is in accord with Jung's observation about the need of the person to find meaning for his dying just as he sought meaning for his living.

Thus the counselor's role with the patient is not merely that of bringing peace but also meaning and order to the events that are experienced. The counselor is trying to do something, and he is doing it against time. He must be aware of the needs of the patient and his ability to communicate his feelings, but he is also aware of special objectives that he would reach. He would try to keep the patient from feeling separated and alone in his final act of the drama of life. But, as expected in the therapeutic process, it is important to grow, to expand the personality, so that not only is the patient helped but also the bereaved family, which is sustained by the insight of the patient.

The counselor is always involved at the philosophical level with his patient. In truth, he is obliged to face the meaning of his own life and death, for clinical objectivity will be hard to maintain. The assurance of tomorrow or many tomorrows is lacking. When anyone else dies, as John Donne said, we are involved: "Never send to know for whom the *bell* tolls; It tolls for *thee*."[3] We are fighting against the unknown in ourselves as well as in the patient. We tend to personalize our own anxiety in our relationship to the patient. The physician can seek to bring relief from pain and, in satisfying himself in this role, can escape to a degree the full impact of the problem. The psychotherapist, however, is engaged mentally and emotionally with the patient's whole being, so that he cannot separate himself. Sometimes the psychotherapist makes the rationalization that time spent with the dying is wasted. The dying patient cannot repay the effort. Time may be spent more wisely with the young and the healthy, who can turn their insight to good purpose for years to come. The parental nature of the therapist's role seeks rewards from his well-behaved children who go forth into life readjusted, with the fruits of restored and healthful relationships. The time spent with the dying holds no such promise, for they make their lonely pilgrimage into death with no promise of better things to come. This idea flaunts our belief in the sacredness of personality and shows us to be time-bound creatures, measuring life by the calendar rather than by the values that are achieved through personality growth. Also, it gives a rationally acceptable premise for escaping the responsibility to enter into "the valley of the shadow of death," with all the anxiety and emotional hazard it invokes. Perhaps that is why in our culture few persons except those who have a history of emotional illness or are subject to specialized institutional care have any psychotherapy during the terminal phases of illness.

Perhaps we do not understand fully the therapeutic function of religious rites and sacramental procedures offered traditionally to terminal patients. Probably many things done in the name of religion have more meaning at the subconscious level than we are aware of. Sacraments may have important emotional meaning in overcoming the feeling of separation. They *may*, in a language deeper than words, make the person feel related to an institution and tradition that are the sources of faith. He may feel "in the company of the saints." Psychotherapists are becoming increasingly aware of the importance of symbolic acts as means of saying much in little time. The clergyman represents a different purpose. While the physician cares for the body, the pastor is concerned about the soul.

There is a growing body of clinically observed reactions of patients to sacramental acts that verifies their deep meaning. Roman Catholic priests point out that reactions to extreme unction fall into three categories. First, the patient may become resigned to death. Aware of the fact that the Church has taken official notice of his impending demise, he gives up and dies easily and quickly. Second is the release from anxiety, apprehension, and feelings of guilt, which often produces physical relaxation, with an attendant relief of pain and other conditions associated with spasticity and tension. Third is the production of subtle changes in body chemistry, which produce a change in the medical picture. It is not unknown for persons to experience what is medically referred to as a "spontaneous regression" of the malady following a sacramental act or deep emotional experience.

That these religious rites serve deep and important psychological as well as spiritual needs is verified by the fact that comparable acts with a nonreligious setting often produce similar results. A full and emotionally valid confession often brings great peace of mind. This has been known and used by many religions and cultures. Often the fear of death is the dread of judgment and punishment. This confession should precede and make way for other religious acts, each with its special meaning—the Eucharist with its blessing, its communion, and belonging to the life of the Church and of God. Here the substance of the bread and the wine may be the medium of life eternal. The last extreme unction may be the touch of the blessing hand.

The psychiatrist who helps the patient unburden his soul of deep and shameful guilt often finds this results in a change in the patient's emotional state, with clearly discernible physical benefits. With the religiously indoctrinated patient the psychiatrist must have the humility to know that his work may be to prepare the patient for confession to his pastor, or for sacramental confession to his priest. For the patient whose repeated confession has never been emotionally valid because of unconscious guilt, the grace of absolution which he first receives in sacramental confession after many hours of work with a therapist is often a dramatic and heart-warming experience. This is especially true with the clergy, whose long practice has often dulled for them the emotional validity of the ritual. Sometimes the processes of psycho-therapy open up depths of emotional conflict, which when resolved bring a new will to live.

Therapeutic objectives embrace a bipolar relationship to the patient. One is to learn as much as possible about the nature of the disease and its varied effects on the being, physically and emotionally. This is essential to entering into the experience with the patient. The second is to relate to the larger context of the experience at the point of meaning. Here the superficial desire might be called "patient-manage-ment," that is, the effort to help the patient cope with his experience constructively. It is in this process that the larger and essentially theological phase of the inquiry is achieved. At this point the patient, with the aid of the therapist, seeks to find a pattern, a meaning, a validity to his life in spite of the disease.

The basic theological question always confronts the "Why?" of life. Why was I? Why am I? The concern is not primarily with "Why am I dying?" or "Why did this happen to me?" Rather it is "Why am I a person?" or "What have I been?" or "What did it all mean?"

Often the patient does this exploration on his own. Jung has referred to a woman who had been in analysis which circumstances rendered incomplete. In the last month of her life he was called to her bedside because of what the hospital staff interpreted as a psychotic episode. When Jung listened, he found that the woman was free-associating, and working through her analysis under the stress of illness and her awareness of approaching death. In her closing month of life she found the meaning she had been seeking and died in peace with a feeling that her life was fulfilled and complete.

Here the end result is not merely an achievement of understanding and insight into the meaning of the disease, but the fact that the disease has accounted for a spurt of integration, wherein the patient finds a comprehension of past and future, and moves beyond despair to a deep inner satisfaction. Inner conflicts are resolved and the soul takes control of life. This calls for a wider framework than is usually assumed for psychotherapy, but it does not violate the basic desire to stimulate the growth of the patient. Here the great questions are asked. As one patient phrased it: "As long as nobody asks the big questions, you can ignore them and let them be. But once they're asked, you can't put them down again until you have the answer."

The counselor must realize that in this relationship there are often three persons in the room. A patient pointed this out one day. After a year and a half of therapy his lung cancer was regressing and he was feeling better. He said, "You know, Doctor, the first year and a half we worked together we were never alone in this room. You were sitting in that chair, and I was sitting in this one, and right over there in that chair was the old man with the scythe." Consciously or unconsciously, the counselee always is aware of the movement of time and illness.

The consciousness of time produces a dual pressure that may create unwise interference with the normal process of therapy, which centers about the thought and feeling of the patient. The therapist may be so aware of the hopelessness of the physical situation that he may assume an unwarranted role and contaminate the relationship with a desire for omnipotence. The preoccupation may be with making some sense out of the disease rather than with finding meaning in the universe. When we seek to reveal the order of the beyond self, the cosmos, or "the Universe" as Giordano Bruno speaks of it, all that happens is lifted to a higher level, and a purity of motive and meaning takes the place of the contaminating desires of mortal man. This is the focus of thought that does not endanger the patient by promising too much, but rather lets him discover for himself the values that cannot be contaminated or destroyed by the biological incident of death. Unwarranted assumptions of omnipotence are dangerous for both therapist and patient, for when the counselor promises more than he can deliver, the therapist feels guilty and the patient feels disillusioned and the relationship is threatened or fractured.

Traditional religion, of whatever variety, primitive or modern, has always tried to fit man's experience into a cosmic context. It is an effort to face the basic existential problems of human existence so that there is enough meaning for life to make it possible to accept the meaning of death. Every culture has developed a fabric of rites, rituals, or ceremonials that seek to give to the total being a conceptual framework large enough to fit his dying into it. Then the dying takes its place in the larger meaning rather than obliterating the meaning by a meaningless death. At this point modern psychotherapy and traditional religious thought may be able to enrich each other's understanding of the nature of man and the meaning of his existence. Each generation must form the philosophical meanings that speak to its needs and its experience, but none is complete or adequate until it makes a meaning for life that is large enough to encompass the experience of dying.

It is interesting to note that scientists have pioneered in creating the world view that gives a large context for the individual's experience. Giordano Bruno said, "Out of this world we cannot fall." [4] Faced with death by burning at the stake for his heresy, he affirmed a faith large enough to make the event a verification of his faith rather than a denial of it. Irwin Edman in his poem, "The Soliloquy of Giordano Bruno," [5] portrays the conflict between the cozy little world of medieval science and frightening dimensions of the universe revealed by the discoveries of Copernicus.

> The vesper tolls and I must be at rest;
> But how can I be at rest in this world,
> With all of its conflicting forces?

Then Bruno goes through the cycle of the events that have worked to bring him face to face with brutal execution, and he comes to a restatement of his faith not in terms of the old order and the old forms, but rather as the expression of a communication between himself and the infinite and eternal that says simply, "The vesper tolls and I must be at prayer." This portrays his quest for meaning; a quest common among those who face death and acute suffering.

Blaise Pascal achieved a mystical union with universal forces by a different path but with a comparable end result. He said, "The eternal silence of these infinite spaces frightens me." [6] Then he set himself to discovering a mode of com-

14

munication that could penetrate the silence and find it friendly. The struggle to get beyond the veils of silence and the unknown may evoke the capacity for mystical response, and union with the beyond self can come about not through frenzied calling out but rather by the quiet listening that opens the being to awareness. This is not incompatible with the mood of modern science, where the researcher works continually with things that are so small or so large that they must be forever beyond sensory experience. Also, the language of the scientific specialist has meaning only for the initiated, and the goal is to find interrelated meaning, a unified field theory, to all that is. Here then the scientist is a conscious part of what he explores. And the therapist with the patient seeks to produce the feeling of oneness-with-all-that-is so that physical death should not obliterate the feeling of relationship with what extends beyond sensory experience in all directions.

The experience of death differs in quality according to the meaning of life for the patient. The creative artists, the poet, the novelist, picture man as struggling to find that meaning. Perhaps that is why great literature, so-called tragic drama, takes man to the brink of life and wrestles with the meaning of the event. We are all aware of the special value we place upon the insights that come from the moment when life is driven into a small corner and states its premise in simple, irrevocable terms. When we hear of the last words of persons speaking from their deathbeds, we attribute special meaning to these utterances, because they seem to come from a no-man's-land between the known and the unknown. We look here for some secret of life, some treasured insight, some kernel of wisdom that is not available elsewhere.

Freud believed that in the unconscious there is no awareness of the possibility of one's own death. Unconsciously, we

15

seem to believe in our own immortality. Consciously, we tend to deny any termination of meaning. Perhaps it is only the philosopher or the depressed person who asks, "Why go on? Why perpetuate this meaningless process?" When we face the frenzied anxieties let off by the prospect of nuclear war, as we did in the Cuban crisis, the panic reaction is a fantastic effort to deny the reality of the events that might engulf us. An Indian priest who knew well both the Hindu and Christian tradition expressed his idea at a group therapy session that talked of the meaning of death in this way: "I have no ideas about afterlife. There may be a Christian heaven or a Hindu heaven, or there may be nothing. The Lord has always been with me and he will be with me when I die." The Christian tradition says that "God so loved the world that he revealed an abundant meaning for life that is eternal."[7] The whole idea of the resurrection and Easter is to come to terms with the event of death as if it were not final defeat but the prelude to a final victory for meaning. In the relation with the patient this effort to turn defeat into victory is not just a device. Rather it is a point of focus for the death struggle. It is given dramatic expression in the efforts of religions not to let their leaders die. The mystery religions of Greece share this effort with Moses and Jesus.

The response to the threat of death varies widely with different individuals. Two recent cases bear out this point. One was a woman dying of cancer. She was uncommunicative, remote, and her isolation was almost impenetrable. She waved her family away when they called. One day, after numerous calls from her pastor, she said, "They're doing the x-ray now." Her husband had died two years before of cancer and x-ray treatment was the final form of medical intervention. The pastor said, "Yes, I know." Then she rolled her eyes as if to say, "What else is there for us to say?" and turned her face toward the wall. There was no further word.

This was quite in contrast to the case of a man with a history of heart disease. He came to see his pastor and spent an hour and a half talking about death and immortality. In many hours spent with him previously there had been no similar discussion. Perhaps he had some organic warning, some premonition of the fact that within forty-eight hours he would have a fatal attack. But here the communication was open and free and he expressed satisfaction at the chance to talk of such matters. It was as if he took some time to complete the unfinished business of life before he experienced the event of death.

Sometimes the patient indicates that he is prepared to die, even willing for the event to take place. W. C. Alvarez[8] has made the point that on several occasions he has worked with patients who were slipping into death, but who through a series of heroic efforts by their physician were restored to a full measure of consciousness, and improved physical condition temporarily. In these cases the patients made it known to the physician that they were displeased with the medical efforts. The patients implied that they did not appreciate the efforts in their behalf, which merely made it necessary for them to go through the process twice. While they did not imply that the process was painful, they did make it clear that they felt cheated in being compelled to use their energy for dying when they needed it for something else.

Sometimes the act of dying serves a symbolic purpose. One patient who made a suicide attempt that would have been successful except for the element of chance which intervened regained consciousness with a feeling of great elation. She had fulfilled the demand for self-punishment by the act of self-destruction just as her father had done before her. But when she was delivered from death, she felt free of the obligation to commit suicide. When a member of her therapy group did commit suicide, she was the one person who seemed to understand what death was, and was able to interpret it to others. Her response was to find new value in life. Far from feeling cheated, she was overjoyed that her life had been restored and she was able to face the future released from the gnawing fear that she would end her own life. She had the gift of life with an added dimension. She had faced the terror of the unknown and sensed that it was not so terrible after all. She had offered her life as payment for guilt and when it was restored, she was free of the debt and began to live a new life.

There are times when the terminal process brings a lightness of spirit, as if one had completed a difficult task and was about to take a vacation. The following quotation from Shakespeare alludes to this mood:

> How oft when men are at the point of death
> Have they been merry! which their keepers call
> A lightning before death.[9]

The fear of death seems to exist up to a point where it is fairly close, and then gives way to a kind of peaceful understanding. This is not resignation or merely giving up. Rather it is a dim unverbalized awareness that this is a part of it all and that it does not call for terror or even real loss. This is more apt to be the case with persons who have had a long time to prepare for their death, and is quite in contrast to the attitude of those who die suddenly and acutely, as from hemorrhage, who show excessive terror and acute anxiety up to the moment of death.

These observations make it clear that death is such a personal thing that the basic psychological state of the individual manifests itself in the variety of ways that have been shown. Death is quite a different thing for the older person, who is easily aware of the completeness of his life, than for the young or middle-aged person, who is just as aware of the unfinished quality of his existence. The elderly person is often quite willing to go in peace and he resents interference with the process for which he has prepared himself. He wants to preserve the dignity of his passing, and objects to any invasion of his privacy. The young person clings desperately to life, seeks all the aid he can find, and willingly sacrifices privacy and dignity to that end. He endures pain with purpose, for he wants to live. The older person may be willing to die, and even to prefer death to the indignity of helplessness. The young person usually wants to live and organizes the energy of life to sustain that purpose.

Here is an indication of what the counselor's objectives should be. The older person is helped in his dying to approach the event with acceptance and dignity, with the assurance that he is valued and not alone. The young or middle-aged person faces the same event with different feelings. When life cannot be restored, the counselor helps such a person to accept the fact with a meaning that gives dignity to his life and purpose even to the process that is encroaching on his vitality.

Very often dignity and privacy are more important than pain. A patient recently commented, "I am not afraid of death. But I must admit I am very apprehensive about the process of dying with all of its messiness and indignity." She was saying that she had adjusted herself philosophically to the event but could not adjust herself to a process that violated her need for meticulousness and order. If she could die as she had lived she would accept it, but having witnessed other persons die in the room of the cancer hospital she could not adjust herself to the gruesome ordeal that lay before her. It is interesting to note that she clung heroically to consciousness until the last moment of her life, as if to guarantee that she be in control of the process and protect the values she had lived by.

A similar attitude is expressed by Hans Zinsser, the bacteriologist, who died of leukemia. As a physician he was well aware of the diagnosis. In his autobiography, written in the third person, *As I Remember Him*,[10] and also in a book of sonnets[11] dedicated to his wife, he describes his thought and feelings as death approaches. He expresses gratitude that he had time to prepare himself and his wife for his demise. He was thankful that death did not leap on him "as a beast in the forest" but that he had time to do the things he wanted to do to end his life in orderly fashion. In this he comforted himself as well as his wife.

We have fairly well established the fact that there is a difference between death as a state of non-being and dying as a process. The fact of death is a final inexorable event that overshadows the living of all humans. The process of dying is the point at which the counselors' skills may be directed. We cannot change the ultimate fact, but we can help create the mental attitude that would move a person toward the event with calmness and dignity. This has been emphasized by Viktor Frankl in his book *From Death-Camp to Existentialism*.[12] He wanted to help his friends in the concentration camp face death not like cringing animals but with the dignity that marked them as men. He believed that men need to die as they have lived. The anxiety-ridden person will be anxious about his death. The person who has calmness deep within will meet his death with the same calmness. This would fit in with Gerald Caplan's thesis[13] that in coping with crises persons bring their total being into the event.

Yet here our experience shows that this is not always the case. Other qualities of the personality make themselves known at the end. We have seen persons whose whole lives were ridden with anxiety and insecurity, who were unable to stand clearly for anything without showing conflict, die quietly and with confidence. One might say they relaxed because death seemed to them to be a solution of long-harbored death wishes. In dying they resolved persistent problems of guilt, insecurity, and anxiety. They had used up the energy of life in their inner conflicts and the state of being without conflict was inviting to them. But that may be too superficial an interpretation. Heidegger[14] speaks of the fact that a knowledge that we must die casts a color over all our living. We perform heroic acts, assume noble attitudes, with the awareness of the background music that is always playing faintly in the distance. At times we may blot it out, but there are other times when it swells in volume and tempo, and we cannot be unaware of it.

Nicolas Berdyaev has also stressed this fact over and over again.[15] He says that the fact that a person can think of death, that he knows his years are limited, is continually directing the course of his living, determining the values he chooses. This allows him to penetrate to the depths of his adventure in living with a great deal of meaning. Each person's personal history is, perhaps more than he realizes, filled with the effort to cope with this ultimate fact. The heroic person wants always to be prepared for the heroic death, and just as truly the person who denies meaning to life and retreats to the mood of the nihilist is preparing for his own death by saying in effect, "See, my life has had no meaning, so certainly my death can have none."

This quality of perpetual preparation shows itself in ways that we do not usually interpret as ways of coping with death. For instance, the person who goes under general anesthesia usually wants to have his will written up to date, as though he would feel guilty if he had left things undone. Persons who buy traveler's insurance before taking off on an airplane flight may think they are making a reasonable gamble with the law of averages, but their deeper motive may be to absolve themselves from obligation in the face of their possible death. Often a person will drive himself in creative effort, such as writing the long-put-off book, with the feeling that this part of his life may be completed should there be some unexpected intervention of fate. Perhaps one of the expressions of love is the concern about the effect of one's death upon others, and life-insurance salesmen do not fail to take advantage of this concern as a motive in their business.

This may well be the point where the counselor is able to be most helpful in his work with the dying. He can be aware of this built-in need for completeness within one's self and in relation to others. He can say to each person, "It is not my task to give specific direction to you as you approach death, but I can help you to sing the song that is within you." Here the person beats out the music of his own soul, fulfills the uniqueness of his own nature. It is here that we are charged with employing all our skill and perceptiveness in understanding the meaning of the individual's life as he sees it. This is not a matter of general philosophy or general religion, but rather the discovery of the attributes that make the person the being that he is, with his unique goals, purposes, frustrations, and failures.

There are times when the frustrations and feelings of failure are so overwhelming that they predominate in the picture. So it can be with a young person suffering from a malignant tumor that has marked off the days of life with cruel definiteness. Such a young person may well feel that he has to face his execution unwillingly. He resents this intrusion into his life and feels cheated. He may be bitter and angry. He may resist any effort to seek completeness. Here the counselor accepts the angry feelings but does not stop there. He may provide the means for the patient's making some contribution to mankind during the closing days of his life. Through art materials the patient may be encouraged to pour out all of his feelings on canvas, or through legal counsel to make the best possible provision for those who depend on him. The distinguished psychoanalyst, Ernst Kris, who died suddenly of a heart attack, spent the last few hours of his life dictating a memo to his wife on how he wanted his patients cared for, and providing the important factors that he felt the referring analysts should know. This served a dual purpose, for it not only aided those who would carry on his work but made him feel that he was contributing something of value as long as it was possible for him to do so. But there are times when we cannot find much of this to take hold of. Here Viktor Frankl may be grasping the ultimate fact when he points out that we must believe that our suffering has a meaning even though we do not discover it, and that our faith in the validity of that undiscovered meaning gives value to the apparently wasteful and valueless event. The flower blooms and dies even when there is no one to see and appreciate it. The value is in the fact. The fact is sustained by the belief that nothing in creation is meaningless. Even the life fractured in its relationships and cut down ruthlessly before its time has its innate meaning, and the person in most desperate circumstances can be induced to contemplate this. If it could be done by Frankl in Buchenwald, it can be done wherever men face extremity.

This quest for inevitable meaning even in the flower blooming in the desert is difficult to describe in relation to the human situation. Perhaps a conversation that took place in the dissecting room at a medical school may approximate the human desert. Four medical students were working over a cadaver, the remains of a relatively young person, without family, who died of a cerebral hemorrhage. One student asked, "How would you like to end up on the trash heap like this with four medical students cutting you up?" After some general discussion another student said philosophically, "This may be fitting into some carefully worked-out plan, if you could accept it." A third added, "Yes, something might happen here through the agency of this cadaver that would change the course of life. Any one of us could get a clue here that would lead us later into a signicant medical finding. I may make some discovery that would lead me into my specialization." After a long period of silence another student said, "For each of us this is the next step in life. What we do has meaning for us and so it must have meaning for him, whoever he was." The discussion ended with someone quoting Tennyson:

> That nothing walks with aimless feet;
>   That not one life shall be destroy'd,
>   Or cast as rubbish to the void,
> When God hath made the pile complete.[16]

The unknown is filled with possibilities and the quest for meaning never ends. Symbolically the student was fulfilling some obligation to the cadaver and immortality was achieved in part by carrying on the meaning of the unknown's life in knowledge and medical practice. How this meaning could be communicated to a rebellious young person unwillingly facing death would be a problem of relationship, but the possibility is always present that even in the events that seem most meaningless there is a meaning if we look far enough.

It may be that the counselor has to communicate his faith in meaning in order for the person without faith to grasp it. Frankl makes the point that the therapists must be committed to faith in order to communicate it. Perhaps this is what has been lacking in counseling the dying. The professional has been so accustomed to keeping his feelings and convictions out of sight that he tends to deny the patient what he needs most, the feeling of assurance that comes from a person of faith.

There can be no real completeness in life apart from a

faith that makes whole—not necessarily in physical terms but rather in terms of a completeness of relationship within the self and with others. The dying patient reaches toward this completeness in waiting to finish his life-course tidily, write his will, put his affairs in order, make his confession and his peace.

It is important to keep in mind that this quest for order and the finding of it may be the prelude to real living rather than the ending of it. The counselor must always be prepared for this dramatic occurrence, for he may be instrumental in bringing it about. Illustrating this is the case of a woman about sixty years of age. Her pastor was summoned and told by the physician that apparently she had but a few hours to live. Her first comment was, "I know what the story is, and I don't want to die hating my son-in-law the way I do. What can I do about it?" They jumped into the middle of the discussion concerning her feelings toward her son-in-law. Soon it was clear that the son-in-law was not the person she hated, but rather that because of his national origin he had become the focal point of many strong prejudices that she had long harbored. Each of these was examined in turn, talked through, and resolved. With great relief she said, "Thank God, it was not that dear boy I hated. He has been all kindness to me, but I have been so mean to him I was ashamed to face him." She sighed in her relief and as a result of her exertion in the strenuous discussion and her weakened condition she fell asleep. The family did not expect her to awaken and the opinion seemed to be shared by her physician. But she did awaken and her condition, physically and emotionally, was much better. She walked out of the hospital about ten days later and lived for years afterward. Her family was sure that a miracle had been performed. Actually, in trying to clean up some of the unfinished business of life she had removed a major emotional block that had undoubtedly been affecting her body chemistry. When her confession was made and worked through, the innate processes of life moved her toward wholeness. Her dying, therefore, was not necessary, and the counseling given the dying patient helped to restore life. Here it was not a matter of writing a will but of righting a wrong. Perhaps more often than we realize the activity that is designed to help prepare persons for a peaceful death is a resource to restore useful life.

Confession in extremis has special meaning. It is assumed in courts of law that deathbed confessions have more validity than sworn statements, for they are made in the presence of a final judgment upon life. The confession of a crime is a final good act to protect others from suffering the consequences before the law. It brings together man's need for integrity in the face of his mortality. Even when persons believe they are dying, confess a crime, and subsequently recover, the validity of the confession is maintained, because the patient believed he was dying.

Refusal to confess when the evidence is overwhelming means that the person carries into his act of dying the unresolved burden of his guilt and denies to others the healing relationship that might be afforded by opening his soul. A chaplain in a state penitentiary where executions take place tells of his experience with condemned prisoners. Some come to their final hours and repeat endlessly that they are not guilty. These go to their death with great resentment and agitation, while those who confess their crimes and unburden their souls appear to find release and inner peace. They say in effect or in words, "I was guilty. I have suffered. I continue to pay for my crime. May God have mercy on my soul." Perhaps there is some of this in every human. We are all aware of guilt, and we suffer and want to get things right before we terminate this existence. There is emotional release and inner peace in the process.

Yet some persons are like the outlaw in one of James Branch Cabell's books who at his execution said, in effect, "I know that I have done these things and that what I have done I should be executed for. And yet, really, it seems to me that I am still the young man who strolled innocently—the child who played joyfully—around the walls of this very castle and walked in these woods." He was not guilty to himself. He had not accepted his guilt. He was still the person who had not done "these things." Intellectually he could admit his crimes, but emotionally he could not accept the guilt that usually goes with them. In his bifurcated state he was apt to feel resentment, agitation, and injustice. Perhaps we too find this conflicted mood in those who are dying and want to confess but cannot bring themselves to do so because there are justifications for their actions that protect their citadel of being and they cannot risk giving up these defenses.

Clinical experience shows, however, that it is the feeling of guilt more than any other one thing that separates a dying person from those around him as well as from cosmic support. Perhaps here the validity of a sacramental act, as well as that of a human relationship, which affords forgiveness in general rather than in specifics may serve the purposes of the patient's emotional need. Either of these can bring a person back into the community that has set the rules for the game of life as he played it. And the confession helps to bring organic completeness to life, for the relation to other persons and the community brought forth life, and though the dying is a private and personal act, one seeks the support of his community as he is sent forth into the unknown. Perhaps it is here that a symbol of unjust suffering, such as the cross in the Christian tradition, becomes a way of redeemed life, for the processes of death often entail suffering out of proportion to the guilt a person feels, and it is necessary to justify the extra suffering by attributing some cosmic purpose to it.

In summary, we might say that the counselor with the dying patient has special opportunities as far as time and need are concerned. This makes some patients more accessible, while others retreat from valid communication. We have looked at the attitudes and moods of a variety of persons to try to understand what it is like to be dying. We have tried to indicate some of the ways in which the loneliness, fear, and isolation can be modified. We have tried to point out some of the ways through which we can help patients to develop a better climate for their dying. It is quite clear that counseling with the dying patient is different from other human relationships. It has an urgency imposed by limited time. It has an intensity of communication for both the patient and therapist stand together on the brink of an unknown. All of the professional skills are necessary to make possible effective communication. The therapeutic objectives must be expanded to make it possible for the patient to gain some cosmic dimension for his experience. The goal of the counseling process is to help the patient find in his own terms a completeness for his life, a meaning for his being that is not obliterated by the prospect of his non-being.

TWO

EXPERIENCE IN WORKING
WITH THE DYING PATIENT

The problem of working with the dying is complicated by the natural disinclination to enter into the experience. The role of the therapist in most relationships is effective to the degree that the communication is shared, the language is a common base for mutual experience. With the dying there is an overwhelming resistance to giving up the role of living to enter into the act of dying. The natural barrier set up is difficult to bridge. In this chapter we will try to gather from experience with dying patients what the meaning of the experience is for the person engaged in it, so that the therapist can be better prepared to enter into it meaningfully for the patient.

The medically oriented person has a double disadvantage, for he is professionally committed to life and the preservation of it. The first encounter the medical student has with death is in the dissecting room. Here the relationship is with physical remains, and the life is gone. The physical being is approached with the clear awareness that the things that made him a unique being are no longer evident. From the dissecting room the student is led through years of careful consideration of physiology, the movement of life forces. When the physician encounters his patients in practice there is the understanding on the part of the patient that his physician is his protection against death. When death comes, the physician recognizes his defeat in the struggle for life. This makes it hard to contemplate death objectively.

But death is so inevitable a fact of human existence that it cannot be escaped by devices, and even the physician is daily engaged in an encounter with his own death. A pastor shared the last few weeks with a physician who was aware of his own impending demise. The latter spent many hours giving careful medical evaluations of his condition and its progress. Each day he started with a brief lecture on the nature and the course of the disease. Then, as if he had adjusted his intellectual approach to the physical reality, he would respond to the pastor's question, "And how do you feel about the whole thing?" This response quickly shifted to the personal and philosophical aspects of the problem. It was then that the person-to-person encounter took place, and the physician moved beyond his role as medical authority, and talked about his own state of mind and emotion. For him the medical analysis was a necessary setting of the stage, but it was at best preliminary for the more important business at hand, that of weighing the intensely human quality of the experience. Here the physician was personally engaged in the contemplation of death that is the common lot of all men.

Because it is difficult for the physician to shift from his carefully disciplined attitude, it may be well to look to the experts in human feeling to gain some insight into the thoughts and feelings that crowd in upon life as it moves into its final stages. Philosophers, by the nature of their quest for the ultimate in life, are compelled to confront death's meaning. The writings of Miguel de Unamuno, in *The Tragic Sense of Life*,[1] and William Ernest Hocking, in *Thoughts on Life and Death*,[2] are illustrations of the philosophical exploration. To look death squarely in the face and plumb its meaning is a source of understanding of what life really is all about.

The philosopher's quest for the answers to the major questions of life is shared to a degree by all self-conscious creatures, and is often intensified in contemplating the end of life.

Orozco,[3] in his murals on the meaning of Mexican life and religion, puts in the artist's language the dramatic answers to the life questions, just as Dali in his pictures of the clocks portrays the fluidity and relativity of time. The artist, in his ability to stop time and hold a moment of rich experience indefinitely, is struggling with the ideas inherent in life and death. The medieval artist's grasp of the great theological truth that he believed undergirds living contrasts sharply with the modern artist's efforts to portray the confusion and meaninglessness that emerges in living that is committed to no great purposes.

The sculptor's effort to catch and hold a moment of life eternally is kin to the primitive tribesman's ritual dance that rescues life from death by the communal acts that dramatize the vitality of the living in the presence of what is both fearsome and mysterious, both loathsome and challenging. Life never seems so valuable as when it stands face to face with death.

Tolstoy, in *The Death of Ivan Ilyich*,[4] with an apperception that grasps more than the clinical, gives the movement of a disintegrating life and shows the correlation of bitterness, resentment, and trivial goals with the behavior of the organism that disintegrates with disease and the death that is both wanted and unwanted. The panic and the pain that come with death's approach, and the frenzied efforts to evade and yet embrace death are clearly portrayed. At no point does Tolstoy break the thread of relationship between the physical events and their spiritual significance. He illustrates in moving language the lines of Shakespeare,

> Ah, what a sign it is of evil life,
> Where death's approach is seen so terrible.[5]

Because science functions within the bounds of a limiting method, with laboratory-tested conditions of measurement and control, it is impossible for science to grasp the full dimensions of some experience. So it is that we look to the arts for understanding of certain aspects of life that cannot be crowded into a small corner. Religion, as the art of living with meaning, also throws light on a dimension of experience that copes with death. Malinowski[6] makes his point that all religion starts from the need to control death or the events that surround it. Primitive religion, by the use of sacrifice, tried to gain some control over the mysterious forces that surround life and death. The destruction of lower forms of life in animal sacrifice was intended to placate the gods and thus protect the lives of humans. Incantations and prayers as well as ritualized acts were employed as symbolic acts of self-giving. In Aztec religion the sacrifice of some humans in order to protect others carried the process to its logical conclusion, but the offering of humans produced guilt that also had to be placated. Thus, according to Malinowski, the process became increasingly demanding of both life and man's conscience until inevitable social disintegration took place. Ritualized acts in traditional religion offer sacrifices symbolically both of the Son of God and the lives of the communicants, all with the promise of power over physical death and a promise of a life that is not terminated by the incident of biological death. The use of hymns that do not hesitate to speak of death and credal utterances that face death tend to give a measure of emotional control over the inevitable terminal fact of human existence. The quest for a wisdom that is more than knowledge is rooted in Biblical literature and made explicit in religious practice as it is interpreted in modern terms. All of this is an effort to cope with man's needs in ways that science does not do. In the efforts to explore the mood and need of the person facing death it is important to be aware of the deeper needs that may find symbolic or unspoken expression.

However, recognizing the limitations of the scientific approach and the values of the arts and religion as sources of insight into the human psyche, it is important for us now to explore the body of knowledge that grows from the point where scientific disciplines and artistic sensitivities meet in the study of human emotions and the lower strata of consciousness. The efforts of psychologists and psychotherapists to enter into the experience of their patients, and the perceptions of the discerning pastor, give us understanding of death from the point of view of the patient that can be correlated and made useful for the person working professionally with the dying.

Some of the most useful work in recent years has been done by Weisman and Hackett,[7] who have carefully observed and classified numerous persons and their attitudes toward their own death. They have also tried to understand the varied meanings of death for those who are related professionally or personally to the dying.

Weisman and Hackett[8] speak of death as impersonal, interpersonal, and intrapersonal to denote types and degrees of involvement in the process. The impersonal death is characterized by an "It-it" relationship. Interpersonal death grows from the "I-thou" relationship, while intrapersonal death has about it the awareness that might be characterized by the "I-I" relationship.

Impersonal death is devoid of human quality, and while it is a human being who has died the human relationships are minimal. The medical student at work in the dissecting room keeps this impersonal quality in his work. The dead body is a subject for study, pathological interest, and record keeping. The "interesting case" in life becomes an interesting body in death. Adolf Eichmann testified to an impersonal attitude toward the death of the Jews who were sent by him to their death. Often those who die in our homes for the aged and in state institutions for the mentally ill are treated impersonally. This is partly because the qualities that mark the personality as distinct have ceased to exist long before the terminal biological event takes place. Partly it is because the social ties have been disorganized to the point that no one cares about the person, and so he becomes a being without significant communication or relationships. Sometimes the impersonal attitude is acquired as a protection against too heavy a burden of emotional involvement by the professional persons who care for the dying. The military leader often seeks to protect himself against the burden of responsibility and the fear of death by taking an uninvolved attitude toward what is so prevalent all about him. But even underlying the efforts to maintain the detached relationship there is always the consciousness of a human quality and a personal threat in all death. Here it is the ultimate defeat that is held at bay by the practical device of insulating one's self against the deep feelings that could easily break through. "There but for the grace of God lie I" is never completely eradicated from the consciousness, no matter what bravado and device may be employed.

Interpersonal death is characterized by the variety of feelings one has at the death of another person where the relationships have been significant. It may be produced by the loss of a relative, a close friend, an associate, or even one who stands as an important emotional symbol. The deaths of Rudolph Valentino, Marilyn Monroe, Abraham Lincoln, and Babe Ruth caused strong interpersonal reactions among persons who had no close personal relationships of any kind with the deceased.

The works of Erich Lindemann[9] and Margaretta Bowers[10] have thrown much light on the nature and variety of reactions produced by this interpersonal syndrome. Sometimes it appears as a form of shock, depression, and melancholia of relatively short duration and quite natural. This is usually the case when the feelings are freely expressed. When the cultural restraints make it difficult to externalize the feelings, repression may show itself in physical symptoms that develop months later. These symptoms may appear similar to those of the person who had died. They may dramatically portray the organic effort to cling to what must be let go. There may be excessive drain upon the endocrine system to maintain a balanced body chemistry until there is a breakdown under the strain and illness results. The origin of some forms of malignancy seems to be associated with an emotional crisis following an interpersonal loss experience. This can produce a bleak despair with disturbance of body chemistry.[11] Virus infections also appear to be related to the emotional crises of life.

In addition to physical symptoms there may be emotional crises. Rollo May, in his study of anxiety,[12] analyzed the cause-effect relationships in the behavior of a number of so-called "juvenile delinquents" and found that in seventy-five per cent of the cases there was a death of a parent or parent figure in the early years of the youths studied. Here the feelings of injustice associated with the deprivation are acted out against society. Persons in the middle years who are normally in good health physically may show their emotional reactions by excessive dependence on alcohol or in changes of attitude and behavior. In aged persons the emotional withdrawal from life may characterize their grief reaction. The therapist often traces emotional problems to a crisis in life that brought the patient into contact with interpersonal death. Unresolved, it may lead to suicide, illness, or emotional maladjustment.

For some persons the encounter with interpersonal death produces profound spiritual problems. The nature of the universe is called into question, the justice of natural law is weighed and found wanting, and the fear of personal extinction stimulates magical thinking. The meaning of life itself is challenged by its termination, and often the combination of emotional reactions accompanying so great a deprivation experience leads to despair, depression, retreat from life, and overtly expressed self-destruction.

It is not uncommon to read in the obituary column an item that ends in this manner: "Mrs. John Doe died at her home Monday evening. The medical examiner said the probable cause of death was suicide. Relatives say that Mrs. Doe had been despondent since the death of her husband six months ago." For many persons the spiritual crisis is resolved by the self-directed act that gains control over death by being able to determine it in time and place. This desire even shows itself in the suicide of the condemned man just before his time of execution.

More than we are apt to realize, the encounter with interpersonal death and the reactions it produces, emotionally and spiritually, become the base from which the individual encounters intrapersonal death. The mental and emotional conditioning concerning death begin to be furnished early in life and continue to coagulate about the germinal idea until a body of thought and feeling develops that engulfs the whole consciousness, and from this the person moves into his own acceptance or rejection of the experience of death.

This leads us to an examination of the meaning and variety of the type of death we identify as intrapersonal, the "I-I" encounter that takes place within the consciousness of the individual as the conflict between being and non-being is contemplated, experienced, and fulfilled.

Weisman and Hackett point out the double meaning of intrapersonal death attitudes: "Intrapersonal death has double significance in that it applies both to the process of dying, particularly the fear of dying, and to the fact of subjective death: each has different psychological aspects." [13]

Few persons are completely free of the fear of death, but it is observed that most persons have a more active fear of the impairment of their bodies and of the process of dying than they have of death itself. Extinction itself is less feared than the process that brings about the progressive dissolution of the things that have been considered to be the acts of living. The fear of disease is associated with the fear of dying. The hypochondriac may be expressing fear of dying by a preoccupation with physical processes that actually hastens disintegration. Such persons are apt to be withdrawn from the world and its varied activities and more and more turn inward to a contemplation of visceral sensations. Their heightened sensitivity to this concern for their own organism makes them susceptible to awareness of activity that they interpret to suit their morbid fears. In psychological terms the comparable apprehension is a fear of insanity. The preoccupation with their internal sensations to the diminution of their interest in human relationships tends to create the climate where anxiety grows and the feelings of separation are interpreted as mental breakdown: ". . . for the patient who experiences it in the vivid, private, intrapersonal world into which no one else can enter, the fear of dying is the sense of impending dissolution or disintegration of all familiar ways of thought and action." [14] The external world becomes increasingly unreal, remote, and unaccountably appears to get along without the patient. The aloneness and separation often lead to acute panic or despair, which because of the separation from any effective communication with those around is increasingly turned inward to produce deeper despair and feelings of helplessness.

This is dramatically shown in the sensory deprivation attendant upon cataract operations where the patient who has long been deprived of normal vision, and so has become very afraid of total blindness, is suddenly in complete darkness under the bandage that, for the first few days, covers both eyes. He frequently begins to hallucinate. Occasionally a patient calls out of the depth of his inner resources a visualization of heaven or hell. Only the person who has experienced the intensity of the beauty and transcendental reality of a happy vision in this situation can understand the high suicide rate of those whose visions are demonic. The same phenomena are observed in those who suffer long periods of isolation, as in shipwreck at sea. Those with impoverished inner resources become suicidal or homicidal and die long before they need to physiologically. Others, more fortunate, experience a religious, a spiritual conversion, which leaves them profoundly at peace with themselves.

A normal fear of dying is essential to the protection of life, and much of what our culture produces is the direct or indirect accumulation of the reaction of man to the threats of his extinction. So we have agriculture and architecture, medical science, and safety councils. But when the fear becomes acute, morbid, and so internalized that it is impotent to act in effective external directions, it becomes a contributive factor to organic death. Joost A. M. Meerloo,[15] in his book on panic, shows how the progressive fears in acute form in conditions where action is impossible may lead to organic breakdown and death. Meerloo has described an incident in a London bomb shelter where hundreds of persons died when no physical injury was incurred and all essentials for sustaining life were present, but overwhelming fear disorganized the life functions so completely that death ensued. Much the same type of acute fear may grip persons who think they have a heart attack, and some die with no indication of heart injury. In normal living there is an awareness of gradual depletion of physical strength, adaptation, and adjustment to limited resources. The doctor at a physical examination may say,

"You are in good shape for your age but remember you are not thirty." This reminder stimulates a moderate fear and awareness that has beneficial effects. Many of the infirmities of advanced years are acute reactions to the fear of death that are generalized most of the time but find acute expression that complicates a disease that in and of itself might be of no serious consequence.

Physicians aware of the power of fears use deception to help the patient cope with his physical symptoms without letting loose the emotional forces that would complicate the ailment. Sometimes they give the illness a different name which is less fearsome. Sometimes they say, "You will feel worse before you feel better." However, with the general increase in basic medical knowledge the prospect of deception may increase anxiety. More and more it becomes a question as to how the apprehensions of the person can be explored and directed toward therapeutic goals. Sometimes the fear of deception may be so strong that even the truth cannot eradicate it, and then it is a matter of working with the anxiety directly and therapeutically.

Bromberg and Schilder[16] point out that subjective death is out of the range of possibility as far as consciousness is concerned. When a person says "When I am dead" he is dealing in contradictions. The persistence of the "I" in relation to the beingness of death makes the death incomprehensible or the "I" the continuing quality. Analysis of the content of dreams involving death shows that the problems of life and the qualities of personality continue in the dreams. The suicidal person often is kept from the final act of self-destruction by the thought that "after I am dead I may not be dead, so that the problems I am seeking to escape may pursue me and my second state will be worse than the first." Religious and literary treatments of the subject give crystallization to the inability to achieve subjective death within the consciousness and so there are the projections of heaven and hell and the stratifications of afterlife as Dante portrays them.

But the element of hope helps to contain the fears. When hope is gone the body's resistance to stress seems to lessen. Dr. LeShan tells of two cases of Hodgkin's disease that illustrate this. The first was a young woman who was in psychotherapy and the disease was apparently under control. Except for an occasional period away from work she was functioning well in her job as secretary. Her therapist was in contact with the employer. One day the employer called the therapist and explained that for various reasons it was decided to terminate the employment of the patient. The therapist explained that employment was an important part of the control of the patient's response in therapy. However, the employer was adamant. When she received her discharge, she lost hope, an exacerbation of the ailment ensued, and death occurred within a week. In the other case a man came to a hospital from a distance asking for a special drug that he had heard was effective in treatment. It was administered to him, the swelling rapidly decreased, and he was not heard from for four months. Then he appeared with characteristic swellings and asked that the drug be administered. The supply was exhausted, and after staff consultation it was decided to administer a placebo, an inert substitute for the indicated medication. This was done and again there was a dramatic decrease in swelling and the patient left in good spirits. Three months later he again presented himself for the administering of the drug. This time, however, he did not believe in its efficacy. He had read of a congressional investigation that raised serious doubts in his mind as to its benefits. The hospital had an adequate supply of the drug in question, and administered it as before. This time, however, there were no observed benefits, and the patient rapidly declined and died within a few days. In both instances the element of hope had

40

been destroyed by circumstances beyond the control of the therapist and the negative results at the loss of hope were as dramatic as the positive results had been when hope was an active factor in the emotional life of the patient.

The patient's image of himself appears to be an important factor in the management of disease, especially in the terminal phases. The devout person whose trust in a sustaining cosmic meaning that gives validity to his life has less fear of death, and so approaches his grave

> Like one who wraps the drapery of his couch
> About him, and lies down to pleasant dreams.[17]

The person possessed by a demonic quality of self-judgment tends to act as if his death were a final judgment. This gives to his dying a quality of anguish and agony that is more the product of his emotions than of his organic state.

Heaven or hell may well be projected psychologically by the patient who sees in his dying a judgment upon his living. It may well be that these concepts, which appear in varied forms in primitive and contemporary religions, are the products of the mental life that projects its consciousness into the beyond-life with the same personal measurements that grow from guilt and a feeling for divine grace.

The intrapersonal meaning of death shows itself in many attitudes that appear often enough among patients to be classified. These might be spoken of as the predilection to death, the escape from death, the appropriate death, the normal death, and the denial of death.

Weisman and Hackett have described the mood and manner of the patient with a predilection to death. These persons "without open conflict, suicidal intention, profound depression, or extreme panic, correctly anticipated their own deaths."[18] For them death was desirable and appropriate, not calamitous. Their fear of dying was secondary to the conviction of impending death that was so sure that it not only overwhelmed the patient but also threatened the therapist, and made normal therapeutic procedures impotent. For these persons their bodies have become an intolerable burden, and they welcome the release from bodily problems that only death can bring. This might be because they thought of their bodies as foul and contaminated by nature or by their misuse of choice, or as the unwelcome bond that kept them from moving into the realm of spirit where they could be reunited with those deceased persons who gave meaning to their existence. In these cases life had become threatening and death held the promise of release. Each in his own way was lonely and isolated, and each had the feeling that he was not only to die but that some other human would be an agent in the process.

Weisman and Hackett present a number of case studies that show how the predilection to death works.[19] One man early in life had visited a soothsayer who said that he would die at the age of sixty. Through the years that date with destiny became more ominous and when surgery was required, the man took it to be the agency for his death, and after the operation went into shock which required the best medical resources to overcome. He was convinced that he would die, and though he did not want to die, his whole being was so adjusted to it that he made no effort to resist the overwhelming forces of fate. The shock appeared to serve as a symbolic death and he was relieved of the burden of doom and left the hospital relieved of anxiety.

An elderly man admitted for a surgical procedure on a stomach ulcer was convinced that he would die of the operation. A psychotherapist interviewed the old man and found that his last enemy, one of several, against whom he had waged a running battle for twenty years had died. He lived withdrawn from creative human relationships, steeped in bitterness, anger, and resentment. The failure of his crops was interpreted as the enmity of the gods and he wanted to die and get the battle over. His serenity was unmoved, and even though the operation was a success, he died three days after it of a thrombus that occluded the pulmonary valve. He approached death with conviction but without anger or depression, as if his reason for living was over and he was glad to have it so.

A woman who had had a colostomy considered herself unclean and repulsive. In spite of efforts of others to reassure her and show their devotion she was increasingly filled with a desire to die. Three miscarriages further convinced her of her worthlessness, but as time went on she lived and her husband and other members of her family died. This compounded her feeling of worthlessness, because she felt she had in some way helped to cause their deaths. She felt the burdensomeness and injustice of life, became more withdrawn and anguished. When the therapist interviewed her before further surgery, she said firmly that she would die of a hemorrhage of the lung. She never attempted or considered suicide, was expressionless as if her face were a death mask. Eight days after surgery she died of a massive pulmonary hemorrhage and her final words were, "I am alone."

A teen-age girl whose leg was amputated because of osteogenic sarcoma fell in love with a boy in the ward who had had a similar operation. During a period of a year and a half she showed no further symptoms and the friendship ripened. When the boy succumbed to his illness with severe localized pains the girl developed comparable symptoms. She remained composed, accepting, and spoke of the young man as if they would soon be reunited. She was serene and merely said she would make the most of her remaining days until reunion came. There was no evidence of depression or anxiety. She appeared neither to need nor want reassurance. She anticipated her death without fear or apprehension as if it were both inevitable and under the circumstances desirable.

For the predilected patient there seems to be no demoralization, no evidence of fear; there is rather an acceptance of fate and an assurance that the death that approaches is more a friend than an enemy. Among the patients referred to there was little intellectual sophistication, and no philosophizing. The will to live and the will to die were in such perfect balance that there was little evident struggle, and the facts of physical condition merely verified the emotional state of serene acceptance. This seemed in most cases to make the pain less acute, as if the lack of struggle for life relieved any spasticity that would have developed.

The patient who recovers from an attempted suicide often reveals the same serene acceptance of death in the hours after the final suicide decision has been made and the preparations for causing death are being undertaken. When there is no longer any conflict there is a sense of inner peace and rightness about the act. To the insensitive observer, the previously deeply depressed person is better. The therapist who has once been so misled will seldom be again.

In the suicide and the patient who expects to die of an operation there is frequently found a life command to die—often because someone he has known and loved or read of has died this way.

Both the suicide who seeks death actively and the patient with a predilection who seeks death passively at the hands of a surgeon will be found to be essentially deeply conflicted persons who often reveal a multiple-personality make-up. The anguished psyche, no longer able to contain its deep despondency, has seemingly divided into two or more "selves." The true self is swamped by the parasitic self that has been taken in or incorporated in identification with the loved and hated person who has died or committed suicide.

44

With unresolved grief due to guilt over having been hostile to this person, the incorporated parasitic personality turns with murderous rage against the true self. There is a time of conflict, when help may be sought, then the true self is no longer heard, no longer protests; the conflict is over and death is sought.

Dr. Bowers reports that in working with a suicidal person in whom this process has resulted in the development of a true multiple-personality structure, she found the hate of the malignant personality for the other selves to be a terrifying experience. The malignant personality accused, judged, and condemned the other selves with a virulent, unrelenting venom, and in the end succeeded after many suicidal failures.

Quite different in attitude and reaction is the person who rejects the idea of his dying and tries to escape from death. He may show his efforts to control death by magical thinking, suicide, stark terror, or religious solace. Common emotional needs exist in the varied devices used to escape death.

The suicide uses part of the self to destroy another part. It may be an anguished psyche, an intolerable psychosocial stress, or a pain-wracked body. One part of the mental process under stress uses another part to blot out the source of offense. But usually before this is done a variety of communications, which Shneiderman and Farberow interpret in *The Cry for Help*,[20] are made that invite aid. Often the communications are oblique and require skilled interpretation to get the meaning, but they are nonetheless efforts to gain aid for the part of the being that makes the total process of living a threat and hazard.

Karl Menninger, in *Man Against Himself*,[21] shows how many and varied may be the ways that are employed by persons who perform acts against themselves. His classification describes three types of action against the self that includes the unconscious and indirect as well as the subtle and overt acts. The chronic suicide is continually engaged in acts against himself, even though these acts may be thought of as quite different by the person involved. The heavy smoker, the drug addict, or the chronic user of alcohol deliberately destroys his life a bit at a time. He knows the consequences of his acts but chooses to continue to do what is injurious. The daredevil, the automobile racer, the boxer, the person who chooses a dangerous occupation, each in his own way invites the hazard wherein death lurks for reasons that are emotionally significant to him. Asceticism and martyrdom would come under this classification, as well as the antisocial behavior that is self-destroying, and the psychotic behavior that is life-denying.

Focal suicide would be more direct and conscious, although still not necessarily fatal. This would include self-mutilation, which destroys a part of the being to save the rest. In warfare the self-inflicted injury is quite common as a device to protect the individual from the hazard of total extinction. Surgeons are often aware of the use of an operation on the part of patients as a way of overcoming feelings of guilt that are intolerable. In a society where guilt is attached to sex activity the surgery of sex organs often represents a sacrifice of part of the physical self to satisfy emotional needs of the total self. In this connection impotence and frigidity tend to serve the same purpose as a denial of part of life's satisfaction in return for the resolving of sex guilt. Students of highway safety note that many accidents occur under the stress of such emotions as anger or resentment and a majority of accidents are attributed to a small percentage of the population who are accident prone. Again the subconscious necessity of emotion cannot be discounted in these cases. In the focal suicide the being appears to be bargaining with himself in a way that trades physical injury, as a price for emotional satisfaction, for atonement. In other cases death is experienced

46

as the only atonement, in still others physical injury or a mutilating operation may be sufficient atonement.

In organic suicide a deeper level of the consciousness appears to be at work. Here the deeply repressed feelings show themselves in a variety of psychogenic ailments. A psychological study of a group of women suffering from cancer of the breast and uterus reveals that they tended to be persons who unconsciously resented and rejected their female role in life. Disease that is sometimes attributed to a hereditary factor may well be explained by a deep emotional preconditioning that expects certain physical conditions to develop and in time furnish the emotional preoccupation that is equivalent to chronic self-hypnosis. What is observed in physical disease may also show itself in mental or emotional illness. Flanders Dunbar, in *Emotions and Bodily Changes*,[22] brings together much clinical material that shows the impact of deeply imbedded emotional drives that are so effective that they outweigh the medical resources that are brought to bear to correct their physical manifestations. While organic suicide may not be the ultimate cause of death, it is a persistent factor in self-destructive activity at the organic level.

Recent studies of the repressed and overt suicide agree that the deep desire is not so much to destroy life completely as to use part of the self to overcome the offending portion of the being. Sometimes it may be a projected part of the being that is socially offended. Then the destructive act is to injure society and its members through the use of the self, as if to say, "I will make you feel guilty for what I do to myself." Sometimes the suicidal act has cosmic implications, as if the person were saying, "You created me and have made my life so miserable I will reject the gift of life to show you how I feel about the injustice and futility of life." The suicide always appears to be denying subjective death, even in the act of inflicting objective death. So it always has about it the element of escape, though the escape is as unreal as the subjective object that remains ever elusive of consciousness and essentially irrational in its expression.

Among those who are terrorized by the prospect of death there is often an escape into magical thinking. Sometimes this is encouraged by the implication of miraculous qualities for religious rituals. At other times persons will be overwhelmed by the claims of religious sects who promise healing or evidence for spiritual survival. The promise of salvation which most religious groups hold up to their members is particularly inviting to those who face death. It can be the device of escape from the threatened self to the beyond self which guarantees cosmic meaning and sustained relationships even beyond death. The variety of ways through which this religious escape is made explicit are too numerous to be examined individually. They appear to have a common meaning for the dying patient as an acceptable commitment of a part of the self to the ideas that will guarantee the survival of the being beyond the moment of physical disorganization.

Weisman and Hackett[23] examine the meaning of what they call appropriate death. This concept is usually associated with a way of life. The captain who chooses to go down with his ship, the kamikaze pilot who rides his plane into its target, the philosopher who drinks the hemlock rather than compromise his way of life, the religious leader who accepts a cross rather than an altering of the values by which he lived, all share this idea of an appropriate death. In each case the feeling of the appropriate nature of the death objectively seems to rob death of its subjective terror. "Quite apart from the process of dying, the concept of an appropriate death is consistent with the hypothesis that our attitude toward our own death is a phantasy of idealized survival in a condensed or disguised form."

The element of martyrdom is probably more prevalent in

viewing objective death than we realize. The patient who welcomes death rather than to become a burden to others is an illustration of this undramatic facing of physical extinction. The political or social leader who risks assassination for a cause also carries within himself the germ of martyrdom as an appropriate continuation in death of a way of life.

What makes one death appropriate and another death tragic? It is strange that, while medicine presides daily over unnumbered deaths and psychiatrists study the psychopathology of death in its protean forms, death has so universally been regarded as a dark symbol beyond investigation. Psychiatrists do not hesitate to study various types of suicide, but the reverse of a suicidal situation, one in which the prospect of appropriate resolution in death far outweighs the fear of dissolution by dying, is rarely mentioned.

Part of the answer to this is to be found in the aversion among doctors to confront themselves with the fact of their own death and to wonder if death can ever be appropriate for them. Despair wears many masks; a hard shell of materialism may cover a tenderness that shuns exposure. The dedication to forestall death is an indication that the medical profession believes that death is never appropriate. . . .

The concept of an appropriate death is one so alien to most people that it is difficult to obtain an accurate appraisal of the circumstances in which an individual patient would be prepared to die. Although he faces the fact that living comes to an end, he finds it easier to imagine the conditions under which he might commit suicide. What responses would most people make if they were asked to write their own eulogies? Would it be easier to write a proposed suicide note than an obituary? Under what circumstances, for example, would the reader be willing to die? It is as difficult to propose an appropriate personal death as it is to imagine subjective obliteration itself. Simply to cite desirable examples of impersonal death, such as dying for a cause; or of interpersonal death, such as reunion with a lost love; or even of intrapersonal death, such as resurrection, does not

49

adequately define an appropriate death. All three personal dimensions are necessary if this concept is to have meaning.

Our hypothesis is that, whatever its content, an appropriate death must satisfy four principle requirements: (1) conflict is reduced; (2) compatibility with the ego ideal is achieved; (3) continuity of important relationships is preserved or restored; (4) consummation of a wish is brought about.[24]

Perhaps this idea is more generally prevalent than we might at first assume, for the courageous person seeks to fulfill the four requirements by a courageous death. The dependent person may fulfill his ego ideal by clinging to another person or an institution to the end. The withdrawn, unrelated person may similarly approach his end as a spectator on the sidelines watching with interest what is happening as if it were happening to another.

It is important for us to realize that death may be quite normal. It may involve no specific morbid state, but rather be the end result of a gradual withering away of the vital forces until so little is left that life is no longer sustained. With many aged persons this may be the case. There is little struggle or alert consciousness, and the ebbing vitality flows out, so that the terminal event is quiet, often takes place in sleep, and without severe personal or social implications. Sometimes the patient when faced with medical intervention to prolong life will say "Please just let me go naturally."

At other times the patient may marshal all the defenses against death and to the end shield himself from the fact by a denial of its reality. Here the subjective inability to grasp the meaning of death may be attached to the objective aspects of the process of dying. In effect the patient says, "This could never happen to me." These are the situations where the defenses have to be carefully evaluated and their meaning for the person accepted. The denial of death on the part of the patient usually finds a responsive note in the professional groups who minister to his needs, for they in effect practice this denial generally as a part of their own defensive equipment.

In this chapter we have tried to explore and define some of the varied ways in which death is encountered, both by the dying patient and those who surround him. Our interest has been primarily descriptive, but one cannot read even the descriptive material without being aware of the therapeutic implications that exist. Not all dying is the same, and not all psychotherapy with the dying can be the same. The nature of the person, the emotional necessity that surrounds the events of his life, as well as the emotional equipment of the therapist, have to be considered. In the next chapter we will look more closely at the feelings of the living concerning the dying, and then will turn our attention to the more specific therapeutic meanings of the relationship of therapist and patient in the subsequent chapter.

THREE

HOW THE LIVING
FEEL ABOUT THE DYING

The therapeutic relationship with the dying patient as we view it is broad in its meaning. It includes the meaning of the relationship that exists with the physician, the psychotherapist, the family, and the representative of the religious institution who ministers to the dying person. What the therapist and family bring into the relationship will certainly be a measurable factor in the mood, manner, and emotion of the patient. Yet too often the emotions of the persons who surround the dying patient have remained unexamined.

The therapist, in working with the dying patient, moves out beyond the normal relationships that are involved in the human encounter. He is obliged to expose more of himself in the process, or conversely he must employ more vigorous defense mechanisms. Therefore the counselor has special needs that must be faced and resolved in order to do his work adequately. Even skilled therapists who work extensively with the dying find that they are used up, drained of their own inner resources. It is at this point that the value of the control therapist shows itself. The person who works with the dying must find some therapeutic relationship where he can restore himself, face his own fears and inadequacies, and move beyond them. A whole set of different attitudes and skills is involved in this traumatic encounter.

The threat to the therapist comes at the point where he is

obliged to move beyond the traditional defenses that he wears and to enter into the valley of the shadow of death with the patient, prepared to share his loneliness and his fears. This means that he must abandon the well-learned and useful devices that have traditionally been employed as protective measures.

The physician looks and acts professionally. He has a certain bearing, authority, attire, and equipment that he usually keeps between himself and the direct encounter with the patient. In the hospital setting he assumes the authority of a high priest whose word is law, and who presides over matters of life and death with implicit omnipotence. Death, however, is a perpetual challenge to the omnipotent stance. The dying patient is a threat to the defenses of the physician, and so at the moment of encounter the defenses are made more secure.

The authority that is granted the physician is born out of the patient's cry for help, but when it is misused it becomes a major threat to communication. In order to look at the feeling the physician has toward the dying patient it is necessary to look first at the defenses he uses to protect himself from the patient as a person.

What are the masks that a physician hides behind to protect himself against a genuine person-to-person encounter with the patient?

There is the mask of professional language, where he knows what he is saying but is quite sure that the words he uses have little or no meaning for the patient. Here language violates its function, for rather than communicating meaning it denies it. This may satisfy the physician's needs, but the patient's needs are violated.

There is the mask of cynicism. Here the things that are sacred to the patient are profaned or made common in the attitude of the physician. This may start in medical school, where horseplay and profanity are employed to overcome the acute depression that usually accompanies the first obligation to work with cadavers. This may be made explicit by an effort to deny the reality of the soul, as indicated by the physician who said to a clergyman, "I have dissected bodies and performed numerous autopsies, and I have looked in vain for anything that I could call a soul." That the comment is unreasonable is not nearly as important as the defensive purpose it serves for the physician who said it. To deny the deeper meaning of life is protection against the deeper meaning of death.

There is the mask of materiality. Here the defense is to keep something material between the physician and the patient. It may be an oxygen mask, a stethoscope, or a hypodermic needle. Whatever it is, it becomes a focus of attention which screens the patient's feelings and anxiety from the tenderness of the physician's soul and makes it possible for the physician to go on about his tasks with protection against a full encounter with the patient.

There is the mask of impersonality. Here the patient is referred to as a case or as a disease. A physician asked his nurse to check the waiting room to see how many patients were still there. After she opened the door and looked around the room she was heard to say, "The heart and the lung are still here." The tendency to refer to the disease rather than the patient is a way of taking a hold of only that part of the being where security exists. Within the bounds of his professional competence the physician is in command, and so, like other scientists, he limits the field of his activity. By emphasizing the impersonal the physician can move in and out of the relationship without having his own core of being inundated by feelings that would be hard to handle.

There is the mask of ritualized action. The physician can come in and feel the pulse. This is a point of contact that may be reassuring to the patient without really meaning much personally to the physician. Other rituals prevail in the operating room and the autopsy room. These are structured types of behavior that stand between the person of the therapist and the person of the patient.

The mask of hospital routine subtly strips the patient of those aspects of his life that measure his personality and his dignity. The loss of privacy is usually taken for granted by the patient, but the continual modification of his mode of life is a way of reducing him to something less than the person he was. The newspaper boy enters the sickroom without hesitation, and the nurse and charwoman come and go as if the personal interests of the patient were secondary to the hospital routine. When efforts were made in one hospital to institute a regime where the nurses and others were asked to knock on the patient's door before entering there was strong resistance, for this again increased the feeling of terror that existed when the patient was met on a person-to-person basis.

There is the mask of the "it-it" relationship. When the person becomes a case it is easy for the physician to assume the role of the dispenser of precise medical knowledge. At this point he becomes an "it" just as much as the patient. So, in protecting the self against the genuine encounter, something of the self that may be very important for the therapeutic relationship is amputated. It may be that a basic fear exists in the mind of the physician that he cannot live up to the patient's expectation of omnipotence, and he himself does not feel comfortable in the role that the patient would thrust upon him. In the denial of the full meaning of the relationship a therapeutic extra is denied.

In outlining the nature of the mask that the physician hides behind in working with the patient it is important that we understand the reasons that warrant it both in the mind of the patient and the physician. On the other hand, it is equally important to realize the cost at which such a relationship is maintained on the part of both the physician and patient. When the physician puts off indefinitely the facing of his own fears he moves farther into a world of illusion. This becomes dangerous for the physician when he thinks that the world of illusion is a world of reality and easily adjusts to it. As far as the patient is concerned, he too is removed from a part of his physician that he may desperately need in his hour of personal crisis.

At no point in the patient-physician relationship are the masks worn with such security as in the encounter with the dying patient. Here, in addition to the usual masks, there is the sedation which can be administered in order to take the patient and his unacceptable behavior farther away from any relationship that might exist between him and those around him. In effect, administering a sedation is often tantamount to saying to the patient, "If you must die, please go off and do it quietly while I am not looking." It amounts to a request to the patient to put on a mask that meets his obligation in the "it-it" relationship comparable to the masks the physician wears in avoiding genuine encounter with the person who is ill.

When the therapist lays aside his masks and enters into a meaningful relationship with the patient surprising results may occur. The therapist may find the relationship difficult to bear and hard to manage. He may find himself growing with the patient. One physician, who indicated a phobia against death and funerals, found that the deliberate effort to capitalize on the grief experiences in his own therapy group proved to be personally beneficial. It can readily be seen that a control therapist has special value for the physician who has such fears and has to face them. The control therapist, however, must be chosen with care, so that, rather than merely engaging in acts of mending the defenses, he works the problems through. When the therapist enters into true communication with the patient he moves beyond authority, for he does not have authority over death, and beyond omnipotence, for no one can deny the ultimate fact of death. All stand inadequate before the mystery of it. But in so doing he emancipates himself from the fears that distort his reality sense and actions that separate him from those to whom he ministers.

The confusion of feeling that is felt by the physician is apt to be even more pronounced in the immediate family of the dying patient. Where any strong love relationship exists there are ambivalent feelings. One accepts the benefits and privileges of love gladly, but the obligations and responsibilities are not so easily borne. When the burdens outweigh the satisfactions things are said and done that are regrettable. When a terminal illness develops, the family is apt to be caught up in conflicting emotions and these show in relationship to the patient.

Strong negative emotions, such as hate and resentment, may be revealed in the family when death approaches. Efforts to control the feelings may be observed by the medical attendants. In one family the aged father was dying, and the sons who had had strong antipathy toward their father urged the physician to do all in his power to prolong the patient's life. When after days of intravenous feedings and other heroic efforts to sustain life the father died, one of the sons was overheard saying to the other, "They really gave it to the old man, didn't they?" Ambivalent feelings always produce a certain amount of guilt, and in a terminal situation where the guilt cannot be resolved normally it may show up in unusual family attitudes and actions. Where hatred exists efforts to prolong life may be urged more to resolve feelings of guilt than out of consideration for the patient's well-being.

The problems of communication may be acute within the family. The medical situation may create a conspiracy of deception which involves the family. The nonverbal communication of anxiety may be so significant that the verbal efforts at reassurance are hollow and meaningless. The long standing problems of communication that exist in many family groups may be accentuated when the prospect of death shows itself. At a time when candid and useful talk is most desirable there may be a thinly veiled practice of deception which frustrates both the family and the patient.

Dr. Bowers has reported a case[1] where her clergyman patient was unable to be the comforting, reassuring person he wanted to be with a dearly loved relative who was dying. He could not give up his lifelong dependent need of that relative. In order to help him accept the inevitable, Dr. Bowers asked her patient to read the burial service as if the death had already occurred. The ensuing two-hour session was frequently interrupted when tears made reading impossible, and the patient talked of some memory of his beloved relative. The reading of the actual interment office was the most difficult. At last it was over, and the patient dashed to the bedside of his dying relative and there found himself the man he wanted to be. His grief work had purged him, and he was free of his own needs, so that he could concern himself with the dying one. Communication, which had become so difficult, was now good again, as it had been in happier times, and in the ensuing days this companionship deepened. There was grief, of course, at the actual funeral, but it was sadness at the loss and no longer a raging against destiny.

The panic of the relatives may keep them conflicted between their desire to relate to the patient and to escape from him. Sometimes the family works out a schedule whereby the members take turns in the sickroom, trying as best they can to endure the observed pain of the patient, only to retreat from it to let another member of the family take over for a spell. Instead of penetrating the pain of the patient with understanding and helpfulness they are conscious of their own pain at the sight of the pain of another before which they seem helpless.

Often in cases where the terminal patient is in terror and filled with feelings of persecution the family is particularly threatened. The paranoid condition that often accompanies senile dementia is hard on the family. The patient turns on those who have been closest to him with anger and bitter words. The family is accused of destructive attitudes and even of criminal acts. This throws them into confusion and they are concerned more about their own defenses than about maintaining a relationship with the patient. Here it may be important to aid the family by interpreting the meaning of the patient's behavior in a way that would enable them to transcend it. One explanation, a psychological one, is that the change in the personality of the patient is due to physical conditions which make a person behave in ways contrary to his feelings. He attacks the persons he loves, and accuses those whom he most trusts. Or a neurophysiological explanation may point out that as the arteriosclerotic condition advances, the limited blood supply to the brain forces the focal point of action from the higher nerve centers downward to the more primitive nerve centers, with the commensurate types of primitive emotions. Usually such explanations make it easier for the family to adjust to the behavior that threatens them and complicates their relationship with the patient. The family should at such times be isolated from the patient and they certainly need special help in overcoming the hostility which may cause devastating after-effects.

The average family member has been subject to the general cultural retreat from the reality of death. He has participated in the practice of denial which keeps death out of conversation, or at least out of the language of reality. When he is confronted with a dying person, especially one who has been bound to him by ties of love and family, he is obliged to readjust his thinking and his feeling. At first he may try to continue the rituals of denial that go along with the cultural pattern. He may try to reassure himself and the patient by saying, "Everything will be all right, you have a good doctor and a good hospital." In effect, he says, "In our science, our society, and our magical thinking we will not let death get us." It is difficult to maintain this illusory thinking when the close association with the dying process day after day confirms man's ultimate helplessness against death. Then it may be that a new and healthier quality comes into the relationship, and honesty with the patient makes it possible for true communication and genuine relationship to be established. It is difficult for the patient to have a healthy attitude toward dying when those about him are saturated in unhealthy feelings about it.

When genuine communication is established, the burden of the conversation may well be an examination of the psyche of the patient. It may show up in questions like, "Why did this have to happen to me?" or "What have I done to deserve this?" or "If this is the will of God, I don't want anything to do with God any more." Expressions such as these call into question the philosophical and religious roots of the patient's way of life. The communication with members of the family can have real benefit if they are willing to enter the conversation, expose their own feelings, and work through the problem with the patient. It is often a reassurance to the patient to know that there are some questions that do not have quick and easy answers, and that we all stand before death aware of our inadequacy. As to the idea that illness is a sign of sin and death a form of punishment, this is not supported by New Testament teaching and violates the whole concept of medical practice. If illness were a form of punishment, then the physician would be guilty of meddling in matters of divine judgment. If death were the final form of punishment, then there would be evidence of an indiscriminate judge at work, for all that lives dies, so the logic of the premise is undermined. As to the will of God, it is important to realize that there is a constant conflict between the ultimate will of God, which is true health and wholeness for all that has been created, and the circumstantial will of God, which continually places limitations on the ultimate will through giving man free choice. Man's own carelessness, ignorance, and willfulness interfere with the working out of the perfect design for health and wholeness. In that sense man accepts responsibility for what happens to him, but it is a far cry from the idea of sin and punishment. Sometimes it is the generalized ignorance of man in the face of disease, which can be overcome in part with time and medical progress. In other cases it is the carelessness that comes when we do not apply all the wisdom we have. At other times we deliberately take risks and suffer consequences. Much confusion in the mind of the patient can be resolved by talking through his feelings with those close to him who are mature and perceptive.

The family represents the basic community. The dying patient tends to feel isolated and alone. To be held close by his family during the closing events of life eases the emotional pain. If the family can take a healthy view of death and dying they can stand in close relation to the patient. This may not involve many words. Often the patient without saying anything will open his eyes and look about the room, or will feel the touch of a hand upon his, and will know that in the lonely pilgrimage into death those who love him have not deserted him in their fears but are standing by in their desire to share his life to the end.

Often the family shows its attitude through its grief reaction. The expressions of grief may be more varied than is sometimes assumed. The family may have an anticipatory grief that works through many of the deeper feelings before death occurs. They may be aware of the grief of the patient who feels the anguish of his separation from what he has known and loved. They may also share the grief of the community at the time death occurs. The nature of the grief indicates something of the attitude toward death held by the bereaved. Those who can express normal healthy feelings about life can give vent to their normal healthy feelings when they face the deprivation death brings. Their anticipatory grief may be shared with the patient who stands to be cut off from all he has known and loved. This may be a healthy and sustaining relationship. It may be the basis for expressing deep feeling, resolving problems, and setting the stage for a mature and competent handling of the event of death itself. At other times, when communication breaks down in a morass of fears, the family belatedly expresses its feelings through the funeral arrangements. They may try to express through a costly casket what they could not say in words. They may with dry-eyed restraint go through the funeral events with stolidity and emotional separation from the events. These persons often present a real hazard, for the constricted emotions find other channels for expression and may show up in physical symptoms, personality changes, and emotional maladjustment. Others, who accept the emotional support of the community, may be able to pour out their feelings in a safe and healthy manner. The emotions surrounding the funeral often indicate the nature of the feelings of the family, whether it was charged with guilt and resentment, or was normal and healthy in its expression.

The concerns of the family that gathers about the bed of the dying patient range from the practical matters of money and security to the impractical considerations of funeral arrangements and religious observances. It is not unusual for members of the family to express anger at the patient for dying. The anger is a realistic act of relationship to the facts and in many respects is more sound emotionally than the complete withdrawal from fact and feeling. Often the family wants the presence of a spiritual counselor, and feels more secure if a clergyman is standing by. This is part of the recognition of the fact that in death persons move out beyond the normal physical sources of security and look to the realm of values and meanings for support and security. But whether the feelings are of anger, anguish, or aspiration of spirit, they need to be accepted and understood as the frontier of the person who is seeking to cope with not only the death of the beloved but also the implicit reminder of his own mortality.

As the attending physician and the immediate family are participants in the personal and private drama that surrounds dying, so the spiritual advisor, the clergyman, is a key figure. What he thinks, says, and does becomes important for the physician and the members of the family. But the pastor at the very beginning is in a paradoxical position, for he seeks to represent the divine while being human, and would seek to give insight into the mysteries that are ultimately as mysterious to him as to others. He would speak of immortality while deeply aware of his own mortality. He would seek to explain the meaning of death when he has only conjectures and not answers.

The attitude that the clergyman himself has toward death will have much to do with the way in which he ministers to the bereaved as well as to the dying patient. His fears, his loneliness, his anxiety in the face of death will be apparent in his work with the dying. A number of chaplains working for a state council of churches in state hospitals reported their disturbance in working with lonely, isolated, and apparently abandoned aged persons in terminal illness. In seeking to work through the problem with these chaplains it was found that the main problem was their own unconscious fear that they would some day be abandoned and alone in the moment of death. Some deep unconscious emotion of the chaplains had unwittingly identified with the condition of the patient and so had complicated their work with the patient.

Dr. Bowers, in her book *Conflicts of the Clergy*, examines the motivation that underlies the choice of profession. She found repeatedly that clergymen who had had traumatic death experiences in childhood sought in the ministry a mastery over death. They could perform funerals repeatedly but never be buried themselves. They could stand at the edge of the grave and walk away from it. The repeated symbolic act gave emotional security and the assurance of a power even over death. But the security was only symbolic and the reality of death persisted with the complication of the pastor's role and the threat to his inner being.

Dr. Bowers points out that wherever she finds a clergyman who has deep unresolved fears of death she has a clergyman who is perpetually angry with funeral directors. This anger seems to come from two sources. First, the funeral is the only service the pastor usually performs where he is required by health laws and traditional practice to share some of the limelight with another. Baptisms, confirmations, weddings, and dedications he performs himself, but a funeral requires adaptation and adjustment to the funeral director. The necessity for sharing the stage with someone else damages the role concept of the pastor, who gains security from being the center of the stage in dramatic public performances. The second, and more significant reason, seems to be that the funeral director stands as the uncompromising community representative of death. If one cannot come to terms with death, the funeral director is the final affront to the pastor's unresolved fears and so the object of the resentments and antipathies that cluster about the idea of death as an enemy. If you cannot overcome death, you can at least try to make life miserable for the person who reminds you of your personal failure.

The roots of these disturbances lie deep. A psychological consultant was invited to sit in with a special committee of a state council of churches which was considering some reforms in funeral practice in its state. During a preliminary session the chairman used his position and skills to direct the committee toward a procedure that would in effect eliminate usual funeral procedures. The plan called for the funeral director to pick up the physical remains of the deceased at home or hospital and take them to the cemetery with no accompanying service. No casket would be necessary and the expense would be considerably reduced. Then at a convenient time, a memorial service would be conducted at the church. This, the chairman said, would make it possible to eliminate pagan practices and emphasize spiritual values. After the first session, which ended without any final decision, the consultant met with the chairman and casually asked how he had arrived at his ideas. With complete candor the chairman said that he had lost his father when he was a boy and was not allowed to attend the funeral. The afternoon he spent home alone wondering what was happening to his father was a time of severe emotional injury. When he decided to go into the ministry he attended a seminary and took a student charge. He said that everything went well except funerals. Here he was so uncomfortable that he went at the last minute, had a brief service, and left as soon as possible. Funerals got to be such a problem for him he decided to give up the parish ministry and take a position with the state council. When questions were asked as to why he felt the way he did about usual funeral practices he quite frankly admitted that he wanted to protect other people from having to go through the painful experience he had endured. It was only after considerable further discussion that he was able to see that he was using the public ceremony attendant upon death as the whipping boy for working off his own unresolved grief and fear of death.

Another pastor, whose brilliant mind made him an excellent preacher and a competent administrator, found it impossible to look at his congregation or visit in a hospital. On Sundays he would focus his eyes on a point high above his people and then deliver a scholarly sermon as if it were committed to memory. There was little or no contact with his people. The hospital was a more serious threat to him. At times he would drive around the block many times before driving away in defeat. The discomfort he experienced in a person-to-person encounter with real people, especially sick people, was acute. He had been orphaned early in life, was brought up in a foster home, retreated into books and scholarly pursuits as a means of security, and felt endangered when he left his cloistered atmosphere and had to meet people as they were.

Yet another pastor suffered acutely when he was obliged to administer the sacrament of Holy Communion. He perspired with anxiety as he forced his way through the service with embarrassment and discomfort. In psychotherapy he revealed that his father, a pathologist, had taken him to the laboratory to keep an eye on him when the baby-sitting problem was not easily solved. The lad was an unwilling witness to many post-mortem examinations. While his father thought he was not paying much attention, the boy was painfully aware of the fact that his father was assaulting the sacred precincts of a person with what appeared to be murderous intent. The boy came to loathe his father and feared the time he would be alone in his presence. When he went into the ministry it was to get a relationship with a good father rather than the one he feared. But when the ritual of Holy Communion was encountered, with its emphasis on the sacrifice of the Son to fulfill the will of the Father, his deepest fears were let loose. Only when his deeply repressed feelings were opened to the light was he able to overcome the fear of death which he had attached to a ritualized act. How acute his suffering must have been when he was asked to administer the sacrament at the bedside of a dying patient.

It is as important to examine the masks the clergy wear to protect themselves from the full person-to-person encounter as it is to see the ones the physician wears. Yet only as the wearer can be aware of his masks and tear them off can there be a free and open communication with the patient.

There is the mask of set-apartness. The act of ordination marks a man as a custodian of the sacred mysteries, as if he knows more of the truth than others, and is granted powers that are reserved for those of special goodness. The full meaning of this separateness may be more the investment of the congregation than the assumption of the pastor, but that merely means that extra effort must be made to move beyond it.

There is the mask of ritualized action. The use of formalized prayers and traditional procedures makes it possible to enter into a human relationship protected against the full encounter with the person, because the communication is general rather than specific. Standing by the bedside the pastor may avoid asking "How do you feel about what is happening to you?" by saying instead, "Shall we have a few words of prayer?" The words then become an insulation against the full feeling of the patient, and the pastor can quickly escape into the environs beyond the sickroom, feeling that he has done his duty, but actually leaving the patient even more alone and separated from those who could enter into his feeling.

There is the mask of a special language. Unfamiliar words weighted with traditional use but little personal meaning may be a wall rather than a bridge. The "Thees and Thous" that are usual in prayers are apt to be stilted utterances that move on a plateau of meaning just beyond the reach of the patient. Phrases like "saving grace" and "redemptive power" may have a familiar ring associated with acts of public worship, but they may mean little and say nothing to the patient, for the deeper substance of the words has never been fully employed. They may mean something to the pastor, or they may be comfortable phrases that can be said with assurance that their deeper meaning will not be called in question.

There is the mask of special attire. The special clothing that members of the clergy traditionally wear may afford ease of access in the hospital, but they say "I am different from you" at the moment when it is important to say "In this moment I share with you the thoughts and feelings that penetrate your aloneness."

There is also the mask of business. Some pastors carefully cultivate the idea that they are terribly busy about a number of important tasks and that they break in upon these many duties to pay the dying patient a quick favor by their short visit. The coming and going have a magical quality about them that say, "The fact that I have been here should satisfy your needs," thus easily avoiding the fact that it is what is done that has its special importance.

For the clergyman death is a challenge to his faith just as to the physician death is a challenge to his professional role. Fortunately, there are many physicians and clergymen who have come to terms with death in their own thinking and feeling, and live emancipated from the encroaching fears. These are the ones who can enter into the experience of the dying person, share the moments in a blessed community of spirit, and serve as bridges of meaning for both life and death.

While it is important for clergymen and physicians to protect themselves by an objective view of death, which makes it possible for them to communicate in their own circle, this should not be used as an escape from wise and useful encounter with the patient and his family. Different attitudes, including a light touch of humor, may be valid in different contexts.

The pastor who puts his people first and is not afraid of them or their feelings is the pastor who can accept himself. He moves easily through life with little need for masks or defenses. He is the one who can sit quietly by the bedside for hours without saying a word, for he realizes that there are times when the protection of many words is unnecessary. For these persons even the ritualized acts are not walls, but rather are the avenues of approach that may become the stepping stones into shared feelings and genuine communication.

In a midwestern city a pastor of profound intellect and personal stature was much in demand for speaking engagements. Yet he had it clearly understood when he accepted an engagement that it was contingent upon his freedom from important pastoral considerations. In his mind his people came first. On several occasions he disappointed large gatherings of persons because he felt it more important to sit quietly hour after hour by the bedside of one of his parishioners. His people had great confidence in him, because they knew they were important to him and could get to him and his feelings. When because of his liberal ideas controversy would ensue it was not uncommon for one of his parishioners to rise and say something like this, "The night my wife died our pastor sat quietly with me all night. He felt my feelings and bore my grief. I don't share some of his political or social views, but he is my pastor and I trust him. I'll fight for his right to say and do what he thinks is right."

What we have been saying in this chapter is that those who are by the nature of their profession or relationship closely bound to the dying patient have unfortunately but understandably accepted the general cultural antipathy to death which is prevalent around them. Not only have they accepted it but in many instances they have used the profession as a further protection against the unshielded encounter with the dying person and his feelings.

The cultural pattern needs to be examined to determine its elements of health or morbidity. Everywhere the emphasis is placed on youth, health, and beauty, as if these qualities were the *summum bonum*. Early retirement plans make room for youth to take over increasingly in business and industry. Special villages for the retired and the aging are set up apart from the rest of society as if to say, "If you must get old and die, please go off somewhere by yourselves and do it. The goddess of youth cannot be profaned." Yet at the same time that we place a cultural premium on youth, medical progress lengthens life and a growing number of persons in advanced years are a part of community life. The split this creates in ideas about the self can be unhealthy. A century or so ago nearly every family had representatives of two or three generations in it. The young and the old shared a common roof and a common board and there was a healthful interchange of philosophy and experience. The efforts to separate generations, with a premium on youth, creates false values and denies reality. In effect it tries to say that aging and dying are not to be considered a part of life. The ancient Chinese custom which venerated the wisdom of the aged gave stability to life, but the current emphasis on youthful vitality without stabilizing wisdom places life in jeopardy at the point of sustaining values.

A similar emphasis on physical beauty tries to deny the effects of the aging process. Styles of dress accentuate youthfulness, and even those who are well beyond their youth dress as if they had to pretend that they were escaping the process by which years are added. The arts and devices of the cosmetician are designed to keep the youthful glow, and even cosmetic treatment of dead bodies makes them look years younger than they were when death came. This emphasis on cosmetic treatment of the exterior of the body gives to life a two-dimensional quality that denies depth and meaning at the same time that it glorifies the superficial. Such a process gives little security at the place where the reality of aging must be faced, and tends to create the atmosphere where it is increasingly difficult to create true values adequate to sustain a person in living and in the facing of death. Yet it must be realized that there are times when the mortician's art lends great dignity to the body lying in state. This was evident recently in the photographs of Pope John, lying in state, looking very much his idealized self— with great dignity and reverence.

While the emphasis on health would seem to be desirable, it is limited in value if it emphasizes a view of health that is related primarily to health as a symbol of youthful vigor and not of wise and healthful aging. In a society that emphasizes sexual vitality as a measure of health it is easy to see that a waning of sexual powers is interpreted as a loss of life itself. But the glorifying of sex in and of itself as a source of ultimate values is hardly adequate to sustain a well rounded value structure.

Quite obviously, the attitude toward the dying that is the

product of our culture is inadequate and is often accentuated among those who have professional responsibility for the dying. That the latter are in part a product of our culture cannot be denied, but that their special responsibility calls for a re-examination of cultural determination and the broadening of the philosophy of life and treatment seems necessary. Perhaps this responsibility honestly faced can help to turn the cultural tide in more genuinely healthful directions.

It is at this point that a creative dialogue among the professional groups concerned with the aged and terminal patient must take place. The pastor needs to face the personal threats that plague his ministry to people just as the physician needs to realize that his responsibility to patients calls for more than a physiological and biochemical interest. There is something about the human being that is more than the sum total of his physical processes and social relationships. Any failure to recognize this and take it into account does damage not only to the patient but also to the professional who works with him. The pastor and the physician need to face their fears and failures together in order to develop more effective cooperation as well as a more adequate basic foundation for their common tasks.

Fortunately, there are encouraging signs of this new cooperative venture emerging. Our present shared venture into considering the tasks of counseling with the dying is but one indication of what is taking place. The staff ministry in hospitals, the seminars of pastors and physicians, the changing climate in the social and personality sciences from a mechanistic to a psychocentric view of man, the mystical quality in the biological and physical sciences, are all making their contribution to a broader base from which philosophical ideas are re-examined and treatment practices are re-evaluated. While the present climate of thought and feeling leaves much to be desired, there is encouragement in the varied activity that shows dissatisfaction with things as they are and wants to find a more adequate premise for both theory and practice.

In the field of atomic physics we have come to the place where the achievements of applied science have become a threat to man and society. The prospects of nuclear extinction are so appalling that like the ostrich we are inclined to bury our heads in the sand rather than face the problem. It is not that the theoretical scientist or the applied scientist has not done his work with brilliance. Rather it is that the conceptual base for psychological and social adaptation to the theoretical and applied achievements of the scientists has not been adequate. While the physical sciences have moved into a new phase, the sciences of man and his value have lagged behind. Much this same type of lag is observed in the healing arts. We have been able to protect and prolong life, but for what? We have yet to develop within the philosophical resources of man a view of his nature that is conceptually adequate to use the advancements that have been made in other fields.

The implications of this for psychotherapy are obvious. It is not enough to approach the dying patient with rituals and medical interventions that merely prolong the process of dying. The meaning of both life and death must be considered by the professionals who treat the patient, so that the patient can find personal fulfillment, a fuller self-realization even *in extremis*. This moves us quickly into an area beyond technique. This brings us into a naked confrontation of the existential values that can be achieved both in living and in dying. This obliges us to face our fears, our failures, and our phantasies unmasked and with courage. This brings us then to the important considerations of the next chapter, where we face the implications of our responsibility for psychotherapy with the patient who is thought to be dying.

FOUR

PSYCHOTHERAPY
WITH THE DYING

This chapter is the nub of our book. In it we emphasize some things that may not be generally acceptable. However, we feel that in general practice the ideas have long been practiced but their meaning ignored. We feel that much more can be done for dying patients than is usually done. By this we do not mean that patients are neglected as far as physical medicine is concerned, but rather that their needs as persons are largely ignored. There is even a growing body of evidence that many persons die well before their time because they have lost the will to live which psychotherapeutic intervention might restore.

Physicians in practice operate on this principle. Weisman and Hackett point out that "As a rule, those physicians with the most to offer therapeutically tend to tell their patients that they have cancer. Dermatologists, for example, inform practically every patient with carcinoma, while, at the other extreme, gynecologic surgeons, whether operating upon the breast or in the pelvis, are inclined to evade or soft-pedal the facts. The largest group of doctors who routinely tell patients about their poor prognosis—and one cannot say whether they have a routine way of telling—are the general practitioners, with whom the patient is more likely to have a sustaining relationship than with a consultant." [1]

There has been a premise accepted in medical practice

that the process of dying desensitizes the patient and that he becomes remote from communication. Daniel Cappon states these general principles thus: "Men die as they lived, beset by abnormalities of character and mood . . . Hence they are at least as hard to approach as they were before. The approach to death is usually overwhelming to the ego . . . The general psychobiological accompaniment to dying is that communications within and without the dying person are gradually shut off. Mercifully, psychic death precedes somatic death . . . What one might call the motivational status in dying, bends toward death. Forebodings of death are more prevalent than one would suppose, and depend upon the individual's state of awareness."[2] But the insights of psychotherapists who have taken the time and endured the risks to enter into communication with the dying seem to refute these principles of Cappon. Perhaps it is the unconscious wish of the attending physician that the patient be removed from communication in order to protect the doctor from self-judgment for evading the unwanted relationship.

The growing importance of the meaning of health and illness as forms of organic behavior that reflect the emotional state of the patient may well be a clue to the meaning of death and the process of dying for the patient. His dying is a form of organic behavior and as such is not without meaning for the total being. If the meaning of the behavior can be discerned it may be able so to modify the emotional state that the organic state is changed. The meaning of the elusive but not uncommon behavior of the organism identified as a spontaneous regression may have relevance at this point. When a patient judged to be dying inexplicably returns to health, the meaning of that behavior is important to explore even though it may be difficult to explain.

A patient comatose for days and judged by the medical attendants to have but a few hours to live was visited by his clergyman. There was no sign of recognition on the part of the patient and everyone in the family said that he had not recognized anyone for a couple of days. The pastor put one hand on the patient's forehead, took his hand with the other, offered a brief prayer, and maintained the physical contact for some minutes. Shortly thereafter the patient became conscious, began to eat; in two weeks he left the hospital and lived quite normally for two years more before a terminal episode. In speaking of the visit to his pastor subsequently the patient said, "I knew you were there." Patients revived after long periods of artificial respiration attest to the fact that although they were unable to communicate by even the slightest voluntary muscular control, they were able to hear what was said, and, as if in a dim distant place, be aware of its meaning for them. It may well be that the awareness of the patient and his availability to psychotherapeutic intervention is more significant than is usually supposed.

This accessibility of the patient to intervention may have strong social implications. An elderly Jewish man, hospitalized in a large New York city medical center, was unvisited. It was the medical judgment that he was in the terminal phase of cancer, which had spread throughout his system. He was remote from communication and could not be interested in any recreational activity or occupational therapy. One day a little girl wandered down the hospital hall asking the nurses, "Where is my grandfather?" Contrary to usual procedure the unattended child was not ushered out, but attendants assisted her in her search until she stood by the bed of the elderly man and said, "Here he is." The child was allowed to return, and the patient began to look for her visits and take an interest in life. His symptoms retreated and after a few weeks he was released from the hospital with no discernible trace of malignancy. A hopeless case had found hope, and organic behavior appeared to be related to the changed state of emotion.

A physician sought psychotherapy after it was determined that he had rapidly developing malignancy of the large intestine. Medical authority had confirmed a limited life expectancy, and the patient had sold his practice and was prepared for the worst. Though he said he didn't have much use for the psychological approach, he sought it as a last resort. It was learned that his father had died when he was thirteen, and that the emotional impact of the experience had been overwhelming. He chose medicine as a career to try to find a way to save life. His own son died at the age of thirteen and the physician-father was doubly damaged by this tragic event. The father-son and son-father roles were complicated by powerful and inaccessible emotions. A few months after his son's death the physician had his first symptoms of ulcerative colitis. These persisted on and off for twenty years before the malignancy developed. In psychotherapy he said, "The terrible thing about being a doctor is that you have no one to talk to." For the first time in his life he talked out all his fear, anger, anguish, and cried the unshed tears of childhood and maturity. Soon thereafter his physical symptoms began to disappear. Bleeding stopped, pain stopped, and in three months he gained fourteen pounds. The clinical picture was completely changed, medical consultants confirmed the change, and the physician who was quite well aware of his own condition considered that he was cured and went about the task of re-establishing a medical practice. Some of the remission may have been attributable to cobalt therapy, which was employed early in the case, but the major change in symptoms came not at that time but later, when the psychological intervention took place.

In the conflict between libido and mortido, between the will to live and the will to die, the major factors may be psychological or spiritual. If the will to live is a major factor in recovery from illness, then it is important not to withhold the therapeutic resources that strengthen this will to survive. While time becomes relative in disease, and especially so in terminal illness, the need for a goal in living is never more necessary than when living is most difficult. Viktor Frankl says, "It is a peculiarity of man that he can only live by looking to the future—*sub specie aeternitatis.*" [3] The goals of therapy with the terminal patient are to strengthen the meaning of life, for this may restore life, and if not, it makes for a richer meaning for the terminal events, for in the face of his death the person can rise to the full stature of his being as a person. In fact, he may find it in dying when he never was able to find it in the past events of his life. This is no insignificant goal in ministering to the dying patient. It can be a goal shared by psychotherapist, physician, clergyman, and the family of the patient.

Subtle and mysterious forces appear to be at work in matters of living and dying. Mice infected with disease germs at one time of day will have a mortality rate several times higher than mice infected at another time of day, all other controllable conditions being the same. Some observers believe that the phases of the moon exert an influence upon the life force. Students of cosmic radiation say that the breakup of molecules in interstellar space also has a bearing on life processes and that the seething storm centers on the surface of the sun have a bearing on physiological functions. More subtle functions of the brain, such as telepathy and extra-sensory forms of perception, may be able, for all we know, to tip the balance between psychic states affecting the will to live and the will to die.

At the present time we do not have a useful way of conceptualizing the life and death forces within the individual. We are forced by a wide variety of clinical data to assume that some individuals "wish" to live more than others and that this desire has—at least in certain instances—a definite effect upon the resistance of the body to stress and to disease processes. These data appear to indicate the existence of a "will to live," but it has not been possible to further define this in ways which would be widely accepted or pragmatically useful.

The limits of the effect of the patient's desire to live upon his body in health and disease—are simply not known. All we know is that these limits are much wider than was generally believed twenty-five years ago. Most physicians today believe that the patient's will to live is an important factor in the pathogenesis of serious illness. Many surgeons hesitate to operate on a patient in a state of depression, for the physiological functions are so obviously slowed down that the healing resources the surgeon depends upon are retarded. In addition to clinical data, a wide variety of reports ranging from studies of voodoo[4] to researches of Weisman and Hackett[5] and studies of the effect of personality on cancer by LeShan and others[6] all attest to the importance of the factor.

Although our basic concepts in this area are very far from clear, there are certain things we can say. In the rest of this chapter we will try to outline some of them growing from our common experience in psychotherapeutic work with a variety of patients in a variety of settings.

In addition to the possible effect on pathogenesis, a second consideration in mobilizing the patient's will to live is the personal values of the patient. In the growth, self-exploration, and self-acceptance that the attempt itself brings, the patient becomes a fuller and richer person. He does not die defeated and beaten by life, but is a stronger and more complete individual. The growth of the self is of value irrelevant to the passage of chronological time. If we believe in the value of the individual and the sacred character of human life, our concern does not stop as death approaches. The responsibility of the psychotherapist, physician, or pastor is not limited to certain stages of development. The treatment of which we speak is not so much concerned with elapsed time as it is with created values.

In a special sense we must consider here some of the philosophical problems that we will develop more in detail in a subsequent chapter, but it is impossible to consider human values in any regard without being aware of the philosophical premise upon which we build. It is here that the therapist must come to terms with his own philosophy of life and death, for it is part of his working equipment in his encounter with the patient. His view will have critical consequences for his work with seriously ill patients. The general medical viewpoint that death is never appropriate must be examined carefully. If such a view is held in work with dying patients with its implication of an absolute separation of the meaning of life and of death, it tends to prevent the greater acceptance of life that is the goal of therapeutic intervention. The therapist then becomes more concerned with blocking death than with enriching life and this interferes with the goal he seeks. It gives to his work a negative rather than a positive emphasis. The viewpoint that has seemed to make most sense for us is that life and death are both aspects of the same *élan vital*, the same meaningful existence. Something deeper is at stake here, for who would save Bruno from the stake, Nathan Hale from the noose, or Winkelried from the spears? To do so would have been to separate their dying from the true meaning of their existence. For by living they would have betrayed their values and the meaning of their lives. In working to increase the will to live we are also working to increase the "being," the "person," the "soul," in whatever aspects it is or will exist.

It is important here to see the contrast that exists between the two Greek deities that preside over health, Aesculapius (Asklepios) and Hygeia. The approach of Aesculapius is toward healing the sick person through the medical arts of repairing damage and restoring disordered functioning. Hygeia symbolized that quality of wholeness that moves the person toward the realization of his nature as a health-endowed being. In our work it appears to be an important goal to bring Hygeia to the aid of Aesculapius.

Beecher, in an excellent discussion of the problem of non-specific factors in disease, has stated: "It is rather paradoxical that, while the group of nonspecific forces which surround disease remains ill-defined, it is now possible to deal specifically, precisely, even quantitatively, with some of the components of the group. . . . Thus we can state a new principle of drug action; some agents are effective only in the presence of a required mental state. . . . These matters lead us inescapably to certain ethical problems. When the absence or presence of disease, when the efficacy or failure of treatment can be determined by those nonspecific factors, we clearly have no right to escape the obligation to plan our diagnosis and therapy on a sound basis which takes into account these nonspecific factors insofar as this is possible today." [7]

So it is important to help the patient move toward his own inner nature, his full realization of positive resources, his own potential as a person, not only for its own sake but also that the patient may then be as fully as possible assisting his physician. We can do this by helping the patient to find and accept his own being and path; to sing his own individual song; to play in life the special music of his unique personality. As the individual moves asymptotically in this direction, the fear of death becomes less and less, even though objective physical conditions may stay the same or become worse.

The patient whose will to live is very weak in a catastrophic situation, except where this has been brought about by extreme physical fatigue and debility, is almost invariably an individual whose will to live was weak before he became ill. As Kierkegaard said, "If a person is at one moment in despair, this shows he has been in despair his whole life."[8] The "presenting symptom" does not then give the true picture. If an attempt is made to solve the problem as if it were the result of the illness, it will have little success. Help is really needed in terms of how to live, not how to die. It might seem that it is a strange and wrong time, when the patient is severely ill, to tackle the deep problems of how to make the most of one's being. This is far from the truth. It is only by going as quickly as possible to the real problem of the patient's life, to the questions of his existence that he has been unable to answer in a satisfactory way, that the will to live may be awakened and mobilized. The therapist must show himself, by his approach, not daunted by either the minor problem, the fear of death, or the major problem, the fear of life. If he can make this clear, the patient can frequently begin to move—often with surprising rapidity—in the search for his own strengths and what has blocked them.

The approach makes far more sense to these patients than does a therapy attitude which concentrates on the search for psychopathology and its causes. It gives the patients much more self-respect, strength, and hope. It may be not so much a hope for physical improvement as it is for that spiritual improvement which Maslow refers to as "self-actualization."[9] This is the patient's real concern for himself, the core of his being. One patient expressed this on a Christmas card she sent her therapist shortly before she died. On it she wrote simply, "Thank you for being my ally." She did not mean being an ally against anyone, but rather a friend and ally in her battle to find the meaning of her own life.

Therapy should not raise false hopes. The concentration should be more on the expansion and freeing of the self than on physical recovery. When the patient finds the road to true wholeness, physical recovery may be a by-product. Where the therapist has the courage to say in effect, "We do not know what the outcome will be, but we do our best. The psychological work you and I do here together can only be beneficial in effect, though we cannot predict the nature of these benefits in advance," he will generally find this acceptable to the patient.

A patient may wish to live and fight for life for different reasons. The two reasons we see most frequently are the fear of death and the wish to live. Clinical experience seems to indicate rather strongly that in serious physical illness the fear of death is not a very powerful tool. It does not appear to bind the resources of the individual together and to increase resistance to pathological processes. The wish to live appears to be the much stronger weapon for this purpose and to bring more of the total organism of the patient to the side of the physician. In mobilizing this wish to live we must have goals in the future that are deeply important to the patient. We need an ideal to work toward. Maslow has pointed out that each culture has its ideal individual.[10] These include the hero, saint, knight, mystic, or gentleman. In our time we tend to have given these up. Ours is rather "the well-adjusted man." This goal, however, has little pull value as far as the future is concerned. Who would work hard and long, fight for life, suffer pain, in order to be "well adjusted"? The ideal, however, of the full rich self, the development of one's own being in one's own special way, the freedom to be one's self fully without fear—this is a goal acceptable to our *Zeitgeist* and worth fighting and suffering for. It is literally a goal worth living for. Patients, once they grasp this goal, seem to find it so.

It is not easy or, with our present knowledge, always possible to make this goal perceived by patients who usually have long since given up hope of achieving it. Generally patients who have lost the wish to live already abandoned any hope for the attainment of the self and have generally judged and condemned their inner self and believe it to be unacceptable.

One patient had been told that he had a fatal malignancy and was going to die by a certain date. Under a new type of treatment his cancer diminished and disappeared. As he was about to be discharged from the hospital he said to his physician, "Doctor, you may not be aware of it, but my biggest problem was not that I was going to die. It's what to do with my life now that I've recovered."

With another patient, the following interchange took place:

THERAPIST: Isn't it time you started being concerned about *you* and stopped being concerned about people's reaction to you?

PATIENT: But they're important. That's what I have to do.

THERAPIST: Sometimes one's job is to cultivate one's garden. The garden in one's backyard, in the front, or the one in one's heart.

PATIENT: What's the use of cultivating a little patch of rocks surrounded by high, thick hedges?

THERAPIST: That's how you see your heart?

PATIENT: Yes.

The approach by logic and reason is not, apparently, a useful one. The deep concern and involvement with life that is central to the wish to live is not amenable to this type of therapy. "You have every reason to live" as a statement to a patient may seem to be true, but, even when buttressed with a list of assets, is not very convincing. It was Spinoza who said with deep perception, "An emotion can only be controlled or destroyed by another emotion contrary thereto, and with more power for controlling emotion." [11] The approach must lie deeper in an arousal of faith in the self and ultimate concern with the self. The despair with life must be countered by something as deep as itself—here the therapist's ultimate concern. Only faith in the person is strong enough to deny the faith in despair.

When we speak of faith here as resident in the patient the term is used in the sense Paul Tillich has used it. "Faith is the state of being ultimately concerned." [12] Ultimate concern means primacy; other concerns—in this context the therapist's concern for himself and his own ego, for his hurt if the patient died, for his pride and his persona—must be secondary and sometimes sacrificed. By this faith, the therapist tries to lead the patient to give up his ultimate concern about "success," the opinion of others, his fears and anxieties, and become ultimately concerned about his own inner development. The therapist expresses *Fides quae creditur*—the faith which is believed. To use Paul Tillich's words, "He who enters the sphere of faith enters the sanctuary of life." [13] This, of course, must be real. It cannot be faked. Such faith demands much of the therapist. Then, when the patient catches the faith, when he begins to respond with faith in himself, he begins to live, he becomes a whole being.

Because this is such a demanding effort for the therapist the "patient load" of persons of this type must be kept small. It is far too great a strain on the therapist's inner resources to have more than a few patients that demand this faith. Ideally, those doing this type of therapy should have other types of patients or other types of work to do. It is important that the therapist be aware of his own inner resources and their limits. He must be a person of faith. Once one starts with a patient in this relationship, it is not easy to stop in the middle. It is quite likely to precipitate a strong depressive reaction in the patient if therapy is abandoned. It is better not to start than to start and not finish.

Basic to the arousal of faith is the approach of the therapist to the patient. Moustakas, in *The Self*,[14] has pointed out that the careful person is only one step away from the paltry person. This is but another way of saying that the good is often a hazard to the best. So it is with this type of therapy. It needs intense concentration, almost absolute caring and acceptance, but not carefulness. If the therapist has reservations about meeting the patient fully, the patient senses it and it reinforces his reservations about meeting life and meeting himself.

Basic is an insistence on a real encounter—a genuine contact between the patient and the therapist. This seems the best way to the bray of the ass that awakened Prince Myshkin to life in Dostoevsky's *The Idiot*.[15] If the encounter can be made without carefulness on the therapist's side and without second thoughts, which the patient usually catches, the breakdown of the wall between patient and life has begun.

The honesty of the encounter precludes the kindness that usually is confused with courtesy. This kindness usually not only has self-protective qualities for the therapist but also the implication of a superior position. Empathy is needed, not sympathy. And the empathy must go both ways. One must be in full contact with the patient before the patient can accept being in contact with himself and with life.

Said a patient, after the therapist had answered some questions about his work and had discussed some difficulties and satisfactions he had with it, "Up to now I've been saying to myself that the things you told me were very nice and exactly what I would tell someone else who was in my position. But now I see that you mean them and live them. So it *is* possible."

We might make here an analogy with one other problem that arises in working intensively with schizophrenics. Between the unconscious of the therapist and the unconscious of the patient there is only the therapist's ego. He is in danger of being drawn into a schizophrenic reality. Here, in the type of work we are describing, there must be only one defensive system between the patient's ego and the therapist's ego, and that is the defensive system of the patient. The patient is thus in danger of being drawn into the world he basically wants so much to enter, but is afraid to.

Too often the training of the therapist is designed to insulate himself against this bold encounter. Fisher[16] has written of the training the psychotherapist receives not to meet the patient openly and fully. He tells the story of the schizophrenic girl being seen at a hospital staff conference. When asked, "How do you like the people here?" she replied, "There are no people here. There's just doctors, nurses, and patients."

The naked encounter makes it plain to the patient that the therapist accepts him without reservation and therefore without fear. He can thus begin to question his own fear of encountering himself. Once this full "meeting" has been made, the process of psychotherapy in a more usual sense of the term can really get under way. Only then is it real to these patients. Without this they are often co-operative and work hard at the therapy, but it is all ego action only. It does not touch the person in his vital centers.

The therapist insists that the patient must constantly search his own being for the sources and directions, the channels and paths of his true self. Montaigne puts it as follows: "Everyone, as Pliny says, 'Is a good doctrine to himself, provided he is capable of discovering himself near at hand.'" He reaffirms this elsewhere: "It is an absolute perfection and, as it were, divine for a man to know how to enjoy his own being loyally." [17] The patient needs this sense of his own value and wonder. The proof of the value of this is in its results as one proceeds. The patient tests his feelings as he goes. If the development makes him dislike himself less, understand the world more realistically, feel more and more at home in the universe, the therapy is worth while and moves well. It should be clear to the patient that the goals of therapy are these practical ones and that this should be experimentally verified by him as he goes along. The patient is trained to listen to his inner sources, to lower the internal threshold and listen to the almost inaudible whispers which say, "I enjoy this," "I do not enjoy that," "I like doing this activity." The idea of this "deep listening" sounds naïve, but, as confirmed by our experience, the patient understands it, takes hold of it quickly, and moves ahead with it. It helps to turn the orientation to a genuine acceptance of, and concern with, the self.

In the old tale the wise man said to the king, "*I* am the most important person in your life—because you are talking to me *now*." It is this sense we try to give the patient; the importance of the only moment in which he can ever live—the *now*. Living in the now and being engaged in it makes it possible for the life force to flow more fully. This viewpoint is part of what Jourard writes of as setting in motion "a general hope syndrome" which seems to him to increase the entropic level of the body, raise the level of the spirit, and "move toward wellness." [18]

An important step in the process of overcoming despair is taken when the patient exchanges his static goal in life for a growing and moving one. Usually the goal has been perceived in a static, utopian state. It is much more realistic and helpful, however, to view it as a dynamic process of reception, expression, action, searching, and growing. Patients seem to recognize clearly the difference between these two viewpoints and find the dynamic much more possible of acceptance.

Just as the therapist tells the patient to search and examine his own goals and values, so he, himself, must keep up with the search, examination, and re-examination within himself. It is too easy to believe that the truths we bring to the patient are *the* truth—to become smug and satisfied with our own approaches and answers. This can blind and blunt our own inner awareness, can block the *sensus divinatatis* by means of which we try to perceive the essence of the patient and his universe. Once we cease searching ourselves, we are telling the patient to do one thing while we do another. This is quickly sensed and our effectiveness is severely damaged.

Psychotherapy with these patients should move strongly. The therapist thus shows both his grip on the seemingly hopeless situation and his confidence in the patient. It may help the therapist to keep in mind the historian Toynbee's concept of the overwhelming challenge that the patient has been unable to meet. Life for these patients has been dominated by a problem they must solve, but cannot. The failure of the life force seems generally to be in terms of the failure adequately to meet the challenge of life, except where a terminal physical state has produced overwhelming fatigue. A patient spoke of the five-year period prior to the first noted signs of her malignancy: "If I looked ahead in life, there was nothing I could see unless I kidded myself." So it is important for the therapist to come to grips with this problem as soon as possible. In this he can push harder with those patients who are aware of limitations on time than one would do in ordinary office practice. One can take the patient's pace and willingness to move as a guide and go faster than might be indicated advisably by the patient's life history or the therapist's "feel" of ego strength. In brief, the therapist should push rather hard as long as the patient is not fighting him. Contrary to the belief of many, the approach of death seems to give a much greater ego strength and the likelihood of a psychotic break is greatly lessened *if therapist and patient are in active encounter and both are clear about their goals.*

The following exchange from the seventh session with a patient shows something of the directness and strength with which the goals of the therapeutic relationship can be pursued:

PATIENT: I'm afraid of my cancer. I want to live.

THERAPIST: Why? Whose life do you want to live?

PATIENT: I detest it! I've never lived my own life. There was always so much to do at the moment. So much to . . . I never got around to living my life.

THERAPIST: You never even were able to find out what it was.

PATIENT: That's why I drink. It makes things look better. Not so dark.

THERAPIST: Maybe the better way would be to find out what is your own way of life and start living it.

PATIENT: How could I do that?

THERAPIST: That's what we are trying to do here.

There is a good deal of evidence that deep psychological isolation, the loss of ability to relate and to love, lowers the ability to fight for health. Paul Federn put it this way: "All that is living must be loving so as not to die." [19] Freud wrote: "In the last analysis, we must love in order not to fall ill and must fall ill when, in consequence of neurosis, we cannot love." [20] The need to relate, however, must be solved in ways organic and syntonic to the patient's personality. Attempting to reach solutions in other ways is worse than useless, since it increases the patient's feeling that his efforts to relate are useless and doomed to failure. It brings no feeling of reward and meaningfulness. Further, since the trail is a false one, it increases the energy going into façade and surface, reinforces the self-alienation and despair, and decreases the chances for relating deeper personality levels and behavior and moving the patient toward wholeness and health.

It is often a problem to help the patient to realize how thoroughly he has rejected himself and is out of contact with his real feelings. One patient told her therapist that she did not know what he was talking about when he said she had accepted her perception of her parent's rejection of her and agreed with it. He asked her to recall the incident in childhood in which she had been most unfairly treated and hurt. She did this and was able to recall and visualize it in great detail. At the end of the incident she had been crying alone in her room. The patient was able to "see" this scene quite clearly and even described the clothes she had been wearing. The therapist then asked her to imagine that they had a time machine in the office similar to the one mentioned in the H. G. Wells story. She was to get into it and in her present person travel back to that room at that moment. The following exchange then took place:

THERAPIST: You now enter—as you are now—the room in which the little Arlene is crying on the bed. You walk into the room. She looks up at you. What do you do?

PATIENT: I'd hit her!

The amazement and shock that she experienced on hearing herself say this was the first step toward a major reorientation to herself.

This time-machine technique, borrowed from Arthur Laurents' superb play, *A Clearing in the Woods*,[21] has proved useful with a variety of patients. For the play, with its brilliant understanding of modern psychotherapy and the search for the self, has been a way of opening for the patient an understanding of the process in which he is engaged. It presents artistically, clearly, and with good taste an idea of what the program of therapy involves. Another literary work that is helpful in a similar way is Hermann Hesse's existentialist novel *The Steppenwolf*.[22] Here, on a more subtle and symbolic level, the author does the same thing. One patient said after reading it, "I didn't understand what it was all about, but after I finished reading it I couldn't stop crying for hours. But they were not sad tears, only bittersweet." Later, in referring to the meeting between the two parts of the hero, Harry Haller and the wolf, she told how struck she had been "by the fact that the wolf had such beautiful eyes and was sad. I guess what I've hated so in me maybe also has beautiful eyes and is sad."

Another patient was asked, as it is often important to ask repeatedly, what she really wanted in life. As they might say in Vermont, "If you had your druthers, what would you druther do?" This woman with breast cancer at first spoke only of her illness and her wish not to die. When, however, the therapist asked, "If you were completely well physically, would you want to go on living with your husband or would you prefer living alone?" she started to answer, stopped, looked puzzled, and said with much surprise in her voice, "I don't know." From this point on she was able to go to work more seriously on her psychotherapy and appeared to be in much better spirits.

The basic self in these patients has generally been so rejected that they are either completely cut off from it or else view its wishes and impulses as completely unacceptable. A patient with a deep love of nature, with a great understanding of flowers and gardens, rejected these because she had been led to believe that only intellectual pursuits were valid. She felt that this love for an interest in the world of nature was something shameful and childish. She was in her own eyes inferior because she did not read the latest professional journals and was not interested in discussing abstract theories. Another patient had been a successful actress and only on the stage felt completely at home and at ease. She had given it up, however, for acting was "like children dressing up in their parents' clothes and pretending." Since then her life has consisted of a constant social whirl, endless arguments with her husband, and an empty feeling of uselessness. Another patient had given up gardening because she was depressed over losing too many gardens, in each of which she had invested many years of loving care and hard work. It was as hard for her to dare to love a new garden as to dare to begin to love a new person. Another had a sullen spite reaction to the newly imposed restrictions of a window garden —nothing less than an acre of ground was sufficient for a real garden—so why try?

In a psychotherapy of the type we are considering we are concerned with a freeing of zest and enthusiasm rather than with the causation of mental symptoms. Symptoms are viewed as results of inability to be oneself freely and as behavior patterns which continue to block such expression. Maslow has put this idea clearly: "It seems quite clear that personality problems may sometimes be loud protests against the crushing of one's psychological bones; of one's true nature." [23]

In this work we are not concerned with mental pathology, nor actually with preparation for death. Rather we are engaged in a search for the inner strengths of the individual. Usual therapeutic approaches often spend more time trying to ferret out weaknesses and flaws in the personality. Rather than a *Sein zum Todt* we are oriented toward a *Sein zum Leben*. Patients seem to grasp this viewpoint rapidly and even those with long experience in classic psychoanalytic therapy quickly seem to find the philosophic approach syntonic and stimulating.

Rosenthal, in her article on psychotherapy for the dying, has stated: "One way to reduce the patient's fear of death is to re-arouse his creative impulses." [24] We would only add to this statement that these impulses have often been so withered by life that it is frequently necessary first to find them and then to arouse them. Further, that this re-arousal gives the individual goals in life that are meaningful and real to him, reawakens hope, and appears to increase the ability to bear with pain and stress and organically to fight for his life. This may well supply the nonspecific factors in treatment that Beecher[25] speaks of, and which may tip the scales in favor of life rather than death.

This was especially true of one of our patients. Toward the end she despaired of psychotherapy—it took too long. But a watercolor, a bit of clay to sculpt, a ceramic dish could be worked on and completed within the attention-span of limited strength. While she was so employed her pain would cease, for pain always lessens when attention is diverted and distracted. This was the great (and only) psychotherapy that the hospital occupational therapy staff understood, this invaluable investment in living, in creating beauty. The frequently held art shows were a delight to her, especially when her pictures were not only shown but sold. This had meaning when nothing else in life was meaningful.

The achieving of this grasp on true selfhood may be aided by helping the patient turn from his overwhelming concern with the opinions of others to concern with the needs of the self. Jung[26] says that often this change takes place in what he calls a second adolescence, somewhere between the years of thirty-five and forty-five. Here the patient discovers the fact that he is a person in his own right. Those who have made this discovery either do not need this type of psychotherapy or move rapidly in it. They are already with life and for it and a part of it. Those who need help in the catastrophic situation are those large numbers of individuals who have not made this important discovery. To them the opinions of others, the "shoulds" of life as Karen Horney[27] uses the term, still come first. It is this neglect of the inner development that seems related to the weakness of the will to live. When they are able to turn their efforts inward, to discover the self they can love, then the will to live seems to increase.

Sometimes the attempt fails. The flame of the life force flickers too dimly. The best efforts of the therapist cannot bring the flicker to a warm glow. A patient with advanced metastatic breast cancer recounted a dream which portrays in dramatic fashion the effort and the failure to be reached. She said: "Something happened in my office. In order to get away from it, I went outside the window and stood on a ledge there. It was very high and I intended to jump. Then someone reached out a hand from inside my office window. I turned to take the hand to go back inside, but it was too late. I tried as hard as I could, I stretched out my arm, but I couldn't quite reach the hand. I almost touched it and then fell off the ledge. As I was falling, I woke up."

Therapists who work with patients in catastrophic situations may find to their surprise that there are real rewards in the work that were not at first surmised or expected. There is a dealing with ". . . . the dimension of seriousness and profundity of feeling (or perhaps the tragic sense of life)."[28] Little effort or time is spent on the superficial, the petty vanities, the superstructure of life. Although strong relationships coupled with realistic dependency are the rule, transference reactions which must be worked through are rare. Usually patient and therapist can come quickly to the basic problems of the human situation.

Further, one discovers something that is rarely mentioned in the textbooks of psychology and psychiatry. One sees clearly the strength and dignity of human beings, the deep altruism, the positive qualities that exist at all levels of personality. Working with people under the hammer of fate increases one's respect for them greatly and makes one proud of being a human being.

Perhaps our point of view could best be presented if we say we are not interested in the dying patient because he is dying, or because he is a patient, but rather that our concern grows out of our belief that as a person he is entitled to be treated as a person at all times and in all circumstances. Even to the end of his allotted physical time the capacity to grow in the understanding of the meaning of life gives a special warrant to this work with the seriously ill or terminal patient.

The approach to the patient that we have advocated in this chapter has raised moral, philosophical, and spiritual issues to which we shall turn our attention in the next three chapters.

FIVE

MORAL IMPLICATIONS
IN COUNSELING THE DYING

Those who counsel the dying patient must examine some of the moral and ethical questions involved in this counseling process. The patient's spiritual and psychological well-being is indeed a responsibility, inviting consideration of the following questions. How can we know what is the truth? How do we gauge the patient's tolerance for the truth? How much truth is the patient entitled to know? How much of the truth can legitimately be withheld from the patient? How is the truth involved in the diagnosis, prognosis, and therapy of the patient? What is the basis for the authority the therapist assumes as he determines the therapeutic role with the patient? What are the legal and moral considerations that must be observed in determining the welfare of the patient? What are the religious and spiritual ramifications of telling the truth to the extent that we know it? How much liberty can be taken with the truth without undermining the relationship between the therapist and the patient? What does the compromising of the truth do to the therapist in a specific situation and to his general attitude toward those for whom he assumes responsibility? Must we move toward new insights and procedures in communication with the patient? How do the attitudes of the new generation of therapists compare with those of the past? These and similar questions now invite our attention.

The range of attitude concerning the responsibility of the therapist for giving information starts from the classic prose presented by Oliver Wendell Holmes in a Valedictory Address delivered to the graduating class of the Bellevue Hospital College, in 1871.

No matter how hard he stares at your countenance, he should never be able to read his fate in it. It should be cheerful as long as there is hope, and serene in its gravity when nothing is left but resignation. The face of a physician like that of a diplomat, should be impenetrable. Nature is a benevolent old hypocrite; she cheats the sick and the dying with illusions better than any anodynes. If there are cogent reasons why a patient should be undeceived, do it deliberately and advisedly, but do not betray your apprehensions through your tell-tale features. . . .

Your patient has no more right to all the truth you know than he has to all the medicine in your saddle-bags, if you carry that kind of cartridge-box for the ammunition that slays disease. He should get only just so much as is good for him. I have seen a physician examining a patient's chest stop all at once, as he brought out a particular sound with a tap on the collar-bone, in the attitude of a pointer who has just come on the scent or sight of a woodcock. You remember the Spartan boy, who, with unmoved countenance, hid the fox that was tearing his vitals beneath his mantle. What he could do in his own suffering you must learn to do for others on whose vital organs disease has fastened its devouring teeth. It is a terrible thing to take away hope, even earthly hope, from a fellow-creature.[1]

The more modern view is reflected in a survey reported in the *Medical Tribune* of May 8, 1961. More than thirteen hundred physicians answered the questions, "When a diagnosis of cancer is established, (1) do you tell the patient the

98

truth, (2) do you tell the patient something reassuring, (3) do you tell someone else in the family but do not tell the patient?" in this manner: fifty-seven per cent said they tell the truth. Forty-nine per cent said they tell the patient something reassuring. This implies that in some cases the truth can be mixed with reassurance. Eighty-six per cent said, "What is told to the patient must fit the individual case." Forty-four per cent said, "The family doctor should always make the decision on what to tell the patient." Seventeen percent said "Patients usually suspect the truth so they might as well be told." Yet when the physicians themselves were confronted with the question, "If you had a malignancy would you wish to be told the truth?" ninety-two per cent answered "Yes." When the answers were classified according to the age of the doctors it was clear that those under forty were more inclined to tell the patient the truth about his condition than were their older colleagues.

This changing attitude toward telling the patient the truth may be the result of patients' increased medical knowledge which makes it more difficult to practice deceit effectively. Also, there may be a growing awareness of the fact that death is not merely a biological event but may also have psychological, spiritual, and social meanings that cannot be ignored. Eissler[2] writes that the patient knows unconsciously that death is impending; somewhere within him there is such knowledge. Herman Feifel[3] supports the theory that death is so much more than a biological event that many other factors have to be considered, and these may be beyond the scope of the medical practitioner. Then too, there may be a changing attitude that the basic human orientation to the truth is more therapeutically sound than an orientation toward illusion or denial, and that sound procedure takes this emotional predisposition for the truth into account.

It is this last point that Weisman and Hackett note in their paper on "The treatment of the dying."[4] They say:

> We believe that the hope and optimism often displayed by dying patients is an exterior maintained more for the sake of those about them than for themselves. Furthermore, we feel that by offering only false hope and optimism, the physician reduces the possibility of true communication and thereby jeopardizes his chance to help the patient.

After some comment on the loneliness of both the patient and the physician when communication breaks down, they add:

> It is a mistake for doctors to assume that all dying patients believe what they are told and accept preferred hope because they desperately need to. There are many patients who value truth in communication and who will lose confidence as soon as trust is violated. The dying patient needs communication and exchange with those around him more desperately than do other types of patients. Dying is lonely, and closeness and warmth are the only remedies. This is our principal reason for advocating truth. . . . The easiest course for the physician to follow in treating the dying patient is to withhold the truth and support the patient's use of denial. There probably are cases where this policy must be used, but we have not as yet uncovered one valid contraindication to the use of truth. The doctor sometimes misinterprets a patient's silence on matters of mortality as evidence that denial is operating effectively. . . . We believe that it is a mistake to assume that everyone feels the same unutterable fear of death. Furthermore, we believe that it is almost impossible to withhold the knowledge of death from a dying person, and that to attempt to do so blindly imposes an unintended exile on someone facing ultimate loneliness.

It may well be that without realizing the emotional meaning of it, the denial of truth to the patient is used more for the protection of the physician in his encounter with death than it is a protection to the patient. The study of the breadth and depth of consciousness tends to support the idea that humans may share some of the same deep and superrational consciousness concerning death that is so apparent in segments of the animal kingdom.

The problem is complicated by the fact that we live in a general cultural period where the nature of being seems to be shifting from a biocentric view of life to a psychocentric concept of existence. Much from the old view still persists, complicating the full awareness of the more recent demands for change. The break-through of insight comes irregularly and the adaptation to new insight does not come as a reversal of practice but rather as a slow modification of it.

Sometimes this new point of view comes from the patients themselves. When a pastor called on a desperately ill patient this conversation ensued: "Pastor, I know I am a very sick man, but I need to know how sick. I can't get any straight answers from anyone here. If I'm going to die I need to know it. This shadow boxing is terrible. You wouldn't lie to me, would you, pastor? What's the story with me?"

The pastor answered: "Yes, you are very sick. But the question you raise is a medical one that I am not competent to answer. But I know how important the answer must be for you. Suppose I talk with Dr. W. about it and see what he says."

The pastor found the physician in the hospital and recounted his conversation with the patient. The physician thought a while, then said: "We'd better have a talk with Mr. T. Come along with me while I do it."

At the beside Dr. W. candidly referred to the pastor's conversation and the questions raised by the patient. Then he said: "I haven't talked with you fully about your chances because there are some things about your illness that puzzle

101

me. You have a stubborn kidney infection that hasn't responded to any of our usual drugs, yet your blood looks pretty good in spite of it and your heart is handling the extra load very well. In a case like yours unforeseen things can happen that may turn in either direction. We're in this together, and we're working on that infection in every way we know. I've told you all I know and I'll tell you if there are any important changes in your physical condition. In the meantime, you and your pastor here can give us all the help possible, for we need it. Ask me any questions you want and I'll give you the straightest answers I have. O.K.? Good enough. I'll be in often."

After the doctor left, the patient said to his pastor: "What a relief to know what the story is. It's terrible not to know and just lie here wondering all the time. One has a right to know about himself, doesn't he?" After a further short conversation the pastor offered a brief prayer for the doctor and the release of the full healing resource within the life of the patient. The patient slept, and the infection retreated. The relief of the patient's anxiety provided by his possession of the truth about himself may well have been a contributing factor.

Sometimes it is the family that intervenes. This was the case with Mr. L. He was admitted to the hospital with persistent nausea and recurrent pain. The condition was diagnosed as an inoperable malignancy of the stomach. The sickroom was charged with an atmosphere of anxiety and apprehension. In response to repeated questions the doctor took Mrs. L. aside and told her of her husband's condition, but said he did not think it wise to tell Mr. L. A couple days later the doctor noted a change in the atmosphere of the sickroom. There was a warmth and closeness that had not been there before. When the doctor commented about it, Mrs. L. said quite openly: "I'm sorry, Doctor, but I couldn't keep your request. My husband and I have never lied to each other and I couldn't begin now. He asked me a question and I gave him an answer. Now the horrible spell is broken. It's better this way. We can take it together better than we could take it separately. Now we can talk about anything, everything is in the open, and we'll share the good and the bad together." And the doctor too shared the feeling of relief.

This does not mean that telling the whole truth as one sees it does not have its hazards. Medical practice is aware of the many hazards that exist. Whenever a shot of penicillin is given there is the possibility of an adverse reaction. The tolerance of the individual to certain medication is always uncertain, and the use of drugs is always contingent upon the individual reaction. The tolerance of individuals to truth also involves variables that can only be established with practice. But with the insights that come as a result of the use of truth there is a growing awareness of the therapeutic benefits that can come to the patient when the imponderables that affect body chemistry are taken into account. But the question always lurks in the background, "Who can really know the truth?"

Dr. Bernard C. Meyer of Mount Sinai Hospital in New York suggests that when the question, "Should the patient be told the truth?" is raised, we ask, "Pray, which patient and what truth?" [5]

The issue of hope is raised as the determining factor in the amount of truth that should be told a patient. This also is a central theme in the writings and comments of many other physicians on the subject.

The *Medical Tribune* of Friday, June 28, 1963, relates how, until the very end, physicians in the Vatican sought to keep the hopeless nature of his illness from Pope John XXIII. This was revealed by Dr. Antonio Gasbarrini of Venice, the late Pontiff's 81-year-old personal physician, when he was interviewed about the patient who had become his personal friend.

"Even if he is the Pope," Dr. Gasbarrini said, "the weapon of hope is used for every patient. We tried to deceive him as long as we could—out of pity—although in view of his strength of spirit perhaps there was no need to do this. We told him it was a "gastric inflammation" but the Pope answered: "I have my suitcase packed:"

Dr. Gasbarrini went on to say that the Pope had an iron constitution and a great faith in the powers of natural recovery and once told him, "I am a bad customer for you doctors."

Dr. Gasbarrini also revealed why regular medical bulletins were not issued during the final illness of the Pope. Pope John was conscious until within twenty-four hours of his death and was able to read the newspapers. His doctors did not want to give him brutal confirmation of the gravity of his illness. The knowledge of the existence of the gastric adenosarcoma was not released.

An admonition often given to those who work with the dying patient is to imbue the patient with faith. As the great neurosurgeon Harvey Cushing is reported to have said: "It will not raise the dead, it will not put an eye in place of a bad one nor will it cure cancer, or pneumonia, or knit a bone; but faith is a most precious commodity, without which we should be very badly off."

In all of our relationships with the ill, the watchwords should be timing, sensitiveness, and understanding. Shakespeare, in *The Tempest*, gives us wise counsel at this point:

> The truth you speak doth lack some gentleness,
> And time to speak it in; you rub the sore,
> When you should bring the plaster.[6]

Especially is timing of enormous importance. In the category of difficult cases the patient goes through a gradual metamorphosis of mental attitude toward his illness, the last step being his realization that he is not going to get well. Of late there are more instances in which the patient is told soon after biopsy that his condition is inoperable and the teller, proud of his honesty, feels virtuous about his truthfulness. Then the teller goes away, and someone else has a serious problem with which to contend, even to the point of despair or suicide on the part of the patient.

In regard to timing, we can learn much from the studies which have been carried out on both natural and man-made disasters. It has been shown that even a brief warning period can enable a prepared and disciplined person to perform effectively when he confronts the disaster. The untrained and less disciplined person requires a longer warning interval and more support to prepare himself. If such findings are relevant to our discussion, then preparation of the patient to receive the truth seems highly indicated.

Therapeutically, one aspect of our work with the dying patient relates to his grief reaction. The loss, or threat of loss, of a loved one will precipitate grief, no matter how implicit the faith in a later reunion may be. While the relative of the dying man stands to lose the affection and companionship of a single loved one, the dying man stands to lose the affection and companionship of everyone. Also, he relinquishes his work, his possessions, and perhaps his chance to see his children grow up. Thus his grief is infinitely more severe and overwhelming. It is not surprising that he has greater need to protect himself by using mechanisms such as denial. Possibly those of us who counsel the dying patient may well take into consideration this grief reaction on the part of both the patient and his family. Then we can work with it in a manner similar to the way we work with the grief reaction in different circumstances.

The Greeks taught that the most horrible of ills is not dying, but dying alone. Thus the dying patient should not be isolated from friends, relatives, or the hospital staff any more than necessary. All members of the healing team should make their regular visits, for the promise of seeing hospital staff members again tomorrow at the same time is a way of saying, "You have nothing to fear in the interim." Though relatives should be encouraged not to isolate the patient, they should not be permitted constant or unduly prolonged visits which the patient may interpret as a "death watch."

Those physicians who state that patients never want to know the truth may possibly, if they take time to listen carefully to the terminally ill patient, see how deeply concerned the patient is over his approaching death. The terminally ill patient may have a recurrence of fear of the dark or of closed doors, of lying recumbent, and of numbness or coldness. The words he uses to express the fears often reveal the primary anxiety: "I am deathly afraid of the dark" or "I feel boxed in when the door is closed."

The terminally ill patient often has an unconscious fear of being "untouchable." The touch or caress is the most basic nonverbal comforting technique we possess and it communicates a solace to the disturbed or frightened patient that words can never produce. Thus the routine backrub or massage given by the nurse engenders both physical and psychic well-being.

No patient should ever be treated as if he had no future. Though a patient is terminal, he should be encouraged to plan for himself and his family, particularly his children. Children are living defenses against the fear of being blotted out and terminally ill patients can derive comfort and satisfaction from the visits of their children and from helping them plan their future.

Many feel that to neglect the question as to whether the patient is dying often increases his sense of alienation and profound loneliness. This point has been made in detail by Tolstoy in *The Death of Ivan Ilyich*. Patients often feel alienated from the family that is not telling them the truth—a truth that they suspect. Physicians such as Weisman and Hackett of Harvard feel that since dying is a lonely business, closeness and warmth are the only remedies. Thus they advocate truth as the correct approach in dealing with the patient.

> We do not mean that the physician must tell the patient bluntly that he has a fatal, incurable condition and will be done in within the month. Truth has many faces, each of which can be employed as it is needed. Nor does truth, under these circumstances, altogether cut off a source of hope. Hope for improvement is never lost, even when a cure is impossible. . . . Truth and hope are not mutually exclusive. . . .[7]

Weisman and Hackett state that often, without knowing more, the patient, actually aware that the family is not being frank, must use up much of his energy in protecting the feelings of his family rather than relying on their support. They believe that to withhold the knowledge of death completely from the dying man isolates him from meaningful relationships with himself, his family, and other persons significant to him.

A sense of community cannot be attained without the patient's knowing the truth and there being a sharing of the truth between the patient and those who visit him.

Most of us have been in situations in which a terminal patient did not know the truth about his condition and our relationship could be nothing more than superficial.

Tolstoy emphasized this in *The Death of Ivan Ilyich*: "What tormented Ivan Ilyich most was the deception—their not wishing to admit what they all knew and what he knew, but wanting to lie to him, and forcing him to participate in that lie. . . . And he had thus to live all alone on the brink of an abyss with no one who understood or pitied him." [8]

A young nurse told of her failure to break through the barrier of aloneness of a patient in the late stages of rheumatic heart disease complicated by a superimposed infection. Each day she entered his room she felt guilty because she was going to live, while he, a man her own age, was about to die. "I knew he wanted to talk to me; but I always turned it into something light, a little joke, or into some evasive reassurance which had to fail. The patient knew and I knew. But, as he saw my desperate attempts to escape and felt my anxiety, he took pity on me and kept to himself what he wanted to share with another human being. And so he died and did not bother me." [9]

The patient will *unfailingly* pick up our fears and anxieties about death, our defense of cynicism born out of our feeling of helplessness in the face of death, and our tendency to withdraw. He will respond in such an atmosphere with a withdrawal of his own, and the opportunity of giving comfort and a sense of fellowship is lost. Robert Frost's sad words then become true:

> No, from the time when one is sick to death,
> one is alone. . . .[10]

One of the most serious obstacles to the care of the dying patient is the lack of communication among all members of the healing team. The doctor usually makes the decision about what should or should not be told the patient, and he usually expects others associated or working with the patient to follow his decision. The patient frequently approaches the nurse for information. She often has the closest rapport with him, for she is on duty in the vicinity of the patient throughout her shift. She could communicate information but often has to withhold it, because the physician says so. This also puts the clergyman in a difficult situation, because he does not know what may be told. Thus he has to work in a setting where depth in understanding and communication can hardly be attained. It is good practice for the doctor, nurses, and other members of the hospital staff, as well as for the family, to make decisions together on how information should be handled with the patient. The physician usually welcomes help with this task.

Even where the policy is to tell the truth there still should be, at all times, good communication among the members of the healing team. As has already been mentioned, truth has many faces. If the approach of always telling the truth is used, there is less anxiety in any member of the healing team about his saying too much. In telling the truth one never has to be blunt and cruel. If the patient is not told that he is terminal, he cannot discuss his thoughts about death with anybody. A conspiracy of silence rules the atmosphere. Therefore all relationships must be superficial and almost meaningless in so crucial a circumstance in a person's life.

Religion is an important factor in what a patient should be told. There is something of a tradition, or at least an approach to this problem, in the beliefs and teachings of the different faiths.

Insofar as the Roman Catholic patient is concerned, the code for Catholic chaplains contains this statement: "Everyone has the right and duty to prepare for the solemn moment of death. Unless it is clear, therefore, that a dying patient is well prepared for death, as regards both temporal and spiritual affairs, it is the physician's duty to inform, or to have some responsible person inform him of his critical condition." [11] According to Roman Catholic belief, at the moment of death the soul leaves the body and appears before God to receive from Him the sentence of eternal reward or eternal punishment. If the soul, when it departs this world, is in a state of friendship with God, that is, if it is in sanctifying grace, it will be saved. If it is in mortal sin, and consequently in a state of hostility toward God, it will be lost. Thus it is tremendously important, particularly for a Roman Catholic patient about to die, that he be given the opportunity to prepare himself for the momentous event.

Most Jewish teachers and physicians have held the view that utmost consideration must be shown for the patient and that his well-being should be the primary factor in determining what information is to be given him regarding the illness. It is in keeping with the religious tradition of Judaism that as much compassion as possible should be shown the afflicted person, in accordance with the realities of the entire situation. According to Jewish scholars, there are innumerable precedents in the Jewish tradition that justify the physician or a member of the family in softening the truth when speaking to the patient regarding the possible or probable consequences of his illness.

The great Rabbi Ben Karshook (immortalized in a poem by Robert Browning [12]) told his disciples they should repent one day before their death. They inquired of him how they might know the day of their death, and he answered that they should repent every day. Possibly the easiest patient to work with in his ultimate crisis is the sincerely religious person who believes that "the eternal God is a dwelling-place" (Deut. 33:27).

The Protestant tradition is not too different from the Jewish. In Protestantism the physician may be looked upon as a kind of pastor, and the wise pastor treats the human beings under his care as he finds them. Probably he will find some patients for whom he must soften the truth that death is near, while others must be treated more frankly. To tell the latter the truth is a tribute to their dignity and maturity.

This subject has legal implications, though little is actually prescribed by law. The law does not say that the doctor must tell his patient the whole truth about his imminent death, nor does it forbid him to do so. The law seems to take a limited view of medical truth. There is no general legal principle that allows a doctor, no matter how high his motives, to tell the patient an untruth with complete immunity under all circumstances. In his effort to know the truth the doctor is granted by law the right to an honest medical opinion. He can err in judgment, and the court will usually accept this. Legally, it is generally accepted that the physician does have the responsibility of allowing the patient to put his business in order. To keep from his patient the knowledge of his impending death would, in certain circumstances, be a very grave error, especially for the family, and the doctor could be held accountable in court for such a mistake.

The truth as related to fatal illness in children deserves special consideration. Often when a physician informs the parents that their child has a fatal illness their attitude toward him changes from considering him a god to looking upon him as an executioner. Children with fatal illnesses are frequently too sick to worry much about whether they are going to live or die. Usually they do sense the fact that

111

they are in grave difficulty and will not live. Not infrequently they read this truth in the faces of their parents and physicians. Sometimes they ask their physicians about the truth of their condition.

The truth can be told to the child in graded doses, and the child seems to be happier if he knows where he stands. This is illustrated by the case of the five-year-old boy described in James Knight's paper on "Philosophic implications of terminal illness."[13] The boy suspected from the tragic expression on the faces of his parents that he was going to die. He asked one of his doctors if this was the case. His doctor told him honestly that he was very sick and that so far the treatment had not been very effective. He asked the boy gently if he was afraid, and the boy returned the question. They both decided that they were not. The following day, when the boy's parents visited him in the hospital, he told them that everything would be all right no matter what happened, and that they should not worry. They asked: "Why do you feel this way?" His simple and moving reply was, "Because my doctors love me."

Usually the child has family and friends around him and does not suffer the isolation and aloneness that many adults experience. Thus he belongs to the group, and the sense of solidarity and community of the group is never broken for him.

We suspect that parents are told the truth about their child's illness almost as soon as the doctor knows himself. Often little effort is made to prepare parents for such dreadful news. One wonders if there exists an assumption that parents can cope with the truth about their children more easily than they can with the truth about themselves.

Those who have worked with children in terminal illness have noticed that children generally accept, without obvious panic, the restrictions imposed on them as the disease progresses. They have less interest in their surroundings as their energy diminishes. Children often ask if their illness is their fault, a punishment for something they did. They must be reassured that such is not the case.

The family's reaction to the prospective death of the child can be compared to separation anxiety. The normal process of mourning usually occurs before the child dies. The family must be allowed this period of mourning, which involves a concentration of interest and energies, self-examination, self-condemnation, and guilt. Parents need to go through these processes, and need the physician's permission to do so. The physician may permit them to voice their guilt and reassure them by the gentle understanding manner in which he answers their questions. Questions frequently asked are: Should I have called the doctor sooner? Did the child inherit the disease from one of us? Did the injury he received some time ago contribute to this illness? Do you think my spanking him may have brought this on? Intellectually, most parents know that these doubts are unreasonable, but they ask such questions because they are so deeply involved emotionally. Ventilation of their anxieties and the physician's reassurance ease their discomfort.

When the parents' guilts have been sorted out and worked through, their energies should be redirected. Both the physician and the pastor are in strategic positions to help in this redirection of guiding them back to the rest of the family. Some parents become active in organizations dedicated to the study and eradication of certain diseases.

Those who work with the dying patient frequently look for rules concerning the road to follow in their counseling. Many who have written on this subject stress that there can be no hard and fast rules regarding the quantity and quality of the truth told to patients. Since there is no standard patient or standard disease it is difficult to formulate any standard procedure for guiding the therapist on the wisdom of conveying to his patient information concerning a serious illness. Neither can there be any fixed policy, for such a policy implies uniformity, and uniformity is seldom applicable to the varied circumstances encountered with terminally ill patients.

Experience has taught us that basic to our work with the dying patient is a sound knowledge of the facts, of the patient, and of ourselves.

As can be surmised from this chapter, we feel that it is usually in the best interest of the patient that he know his condition. This is not always the easiest road to follow in counseling the dying patient, but it is the road that can lead to fruitful encounter and a sense of community in the life of the patient. Such a course of action demands an attitude of sensitive response on the part of the therapist, of entering into the feelings of the patient rather than avoiding or directing them.

Stephen Vincent Benét, in his short story "No Visitors," [14] tells how the hero, John Blagden, a writer, after having had an exploratory operation, discovers during the span of a day the truth about his fatal condition. In this crisis he gets no help from either doctor or nurse. The surgeon answers with evasions and the nurse responds with the "don't you worry" technique. Though Blagden may have been reassured momentarily, he begins to recollect "the tone, the inflection of the voice," to analyze "the fine poised smile . . . the verdict written all over him." At the end of the day he comes to his conclusions: "Why, it is easy to do. . . . They make a great fuss about it, but it's easy to do. . . . All it takes is being mortal." Benét's patient had lived richly and possessed the inner resources to face death as the rounding out of life. On the other hand, the people entrusted with his care did not credit him with the strength he had. In spite of the patient's very direct questions, he had to struggle through it alone, unaided and even led far afield.

We must ever remind ourselves of the dignity and profundity often attained by an individual in his final hours. Such a reminder is contained in a letter from a German soldier to his wife, written in the last hours of the battle of Stalingrad, knowing he would not survive:

> It is strange that people value things only when they are about to lose them. The vast distance is spanned by the bridge from heart to heart. . . . As long as there are shores, there will always be bridges. We should have the courage to walk on them. One bridge leads to you, the other to eternity; at the very end they are the same for me. Tomorrow I shall set forth on the last bridge; give me your hand, so that crossing it won't be so hard.[15]

The increased knowledge we have of the meaning and movement of emotion seems to make it evident that in the healthy person there is a basic tolerance for truth and an aversion to deception. With the unhealthy person the very nature of his unhealthy emotions is demonstrated by a disturbance of his reality sense and too easy an adaptation to the unreal, the false, and the denial.

Perhaps the insight we have gained from the careful study of the deep emotions that go with acute deprivation have relevance here, for death is surely a deprivation experience both for the dying and those who share the anticipatory grief in watching the approach of death.

Here it is important to realize the validity of feelings. Too often we feel false comfort in trying to intellectualize our feelings. This is apt to be the practice with those who are a part of the "intelligentsia," for the very facility with thoughts tends to make the deeper feelings less accessible. Feelings have their own integrity. We feel our feelings just as significantly as we think our thoughts. In situations where deep feelings are at work it is a threatening exclusion from life to have the feelings denied and intellectualizations put in their place.

Events surrounding the approach of death should make adequate provision for the expressions of feelings, both the good and the bad. Anger at the physician and at God is a sign of a struggle for a healthy relationship with reality, and is a valid though uncomfortable feeling. In working through the emotional crisis it is probably better to make it possible for the patient and his family to express their legitimate feelings, rather than to ignore or deny them. Feelings have a way of expressing themselves, sooner or later, in unhealthy ways if there are no healthful channels that can be used. It is never a question of whether the feelings exist, but rather of how they will be expressed.

Perhaps we have an obligation to help furnish the channels through which the deep but normal feelings can be expressed. Then the unhealthy fruits of unwise repression and denial will not plague either the experience of dying or the experience of those who bear the burdens of bereavement. A feeling of community, of shared emotions, and an honest facing of reality seem to undergird life with strength rather than shatter it with weakness.

Since truth can stimulate strong emotions that may have positive bearing upon life, it may be that truth presented with a wise use of psychotherapeutic intervention may actually restore vitality and serve as an aid in the healing process. Questions with deep moral implications have to be asked: How many persons have died because they have been denied the truth and the stimulation of life that reality brings? How much human dignity can be maintained when life is lived in a fabric of subtle deception?

Many of the questions raised at the beginning of this chapter can only be partially answered, for they call for a greater wisdom that we possess. But the importance of communication as contrasted to isolation, the value of a supporting community as contrasted with the loneliness that fear builds around a patient need to be considered. A continued exploration of these problems and a candid dialogue among the members of the healing team need to continue. Also, the growing body of clinical observation should be expanded and evaluated with concern for the person who dies rather than with the disease he dies of. If there is a truth that sets men free we cannot ignore its value. If there are spiritual resources that can sustain persons in life and in death, these need to be identified and used. If there are valid resources of a philosophical and theological nature that can be brought to bear on the critical process of dying then we need to give careful and continued thought to their meaning. This becomes then a moral obligation resting heavily upon those who share professional responsibility in the care of the dying.

To these considerations, then, we will turn our attention next.

SIX

PHILOSOPHICAL CONSIDERATIONS
IN COUNSELING THE DYING

At the beginning of this chapter we should make it clear that we are not concerned with presenting an ordered and definitive or even an entirely consistent system of philosophy. Rather we would point out some of the philosophical dimensions that must be considered when doing therapy with a terminal patient. Here the care of the patient becomes less a precise medical problem and enters more intensively into the philosophical considerations. These considerations may be implicit in all therapy, but are certainly made explicit when the approach of death raises questions that explore the deeper meaning of life itself.

These questions focus attention upon the nature of man, the resources of his mind, the nature and dimensions of his capacity to communicate, a medically acceptable definition of faith, the impact of education on man's view of himself, the meaning of creative selfhood, the quest for values, and the therapeutic objectives that may be attained in the light of this broader study of man's nature. Also for consideration are the existential anxiety that man experiences and the varied ways in which he seeks to allay it. This existential anxiety may come close to the core of therapeutic interest in working with the dying.

All men are rudimentary philosophers, because the concerns of life that affect meaning and value appear to have an innate and socially verified quality. As a living being endowed with consciousness man feels a deep need to examine himself. This, in turn, leads to the search for a reasonable interpretation of life and death. Man tries to understand the meaning of his innate actions and the sources of the feelings that preceed and accompany them. Injustice offends, while justice makes him feel secure. The illogical confounds, while the reasonable fulfils his need for order. Evil threatens, while the good undergirds his response to life. Ugliness offends, while beauty brings him closer to the meanings that sustain life. When we face the various levels of life upon which man may live, we cannot discount that part of our insight that comes with the perspective of the philosopher.

The burden of self-consciousness which rests so heavily upon man is the root of his inner conflict. He can objectify his behavior and its meaning. He can accumulate meanings, which becomes history. He can pass on meanings, which becomes education. In his self-consciousness he craves a freedom he cannot have, because he is continually engaged in limiting it by his history and education. So his conflict is a built-in hazard and resource. It is a hazard because it creates more conflict. It is a resource because through it he struggles to gain freedom through control, and the control becomes the soil from which science, the arts, philosophy, and religion emerge.

One of the essentials of this self-consciousness is the capacity for meaningful communication. When communication is fruitful, the person grows in self-knowledge and creative relationships. When communication breaks down, the person is steeped in the anxiety that leads to despair. The honest communication of the normal person undergirds life with security. Deception with the normal person breeds insecurity, inner conflict, apprehension, and feeling of futility.

One interpretation of communication is found in the four

books of Jurgen Ruesch. In the first, *Communication: The Social Matrix of Psychiatry*,[1] he analyzes the basic problems of fruitful communication. Approaching the problem from experience with abnormal persons he theorizes that the paranoid person wallows in the effects of his self-deception. The schizophrenic, unable to establish normal, healthy communication, retreats into a world of his own for safety, and lives with his own symbolization in a world of unreality. The manic-depressive, unable to find a balance within himself, fluctuates between elated and depressive behavior, which is the acting out of his problems of communication within himself and with others. The neurotic still clings to reality, but is tortured by the effect that it has upon him. He therefore builds up a variety of defenses against the full impact of what life and his experience say to him. The normal person, in contrast, works out the problems of his life in a vigorous and active encounter with himself and his universe, even though at times it is painful. In working with terminal patients the relevance of these classifications is apparent, for the abnormal person would predicate an abnormal approach to death, just as a good grasp of reality becomes the foundation upon which a realistic meeting with personal and family problems can be achieved.

In *Nonverbal Communication*[2] Ruesch, with the aid of Kees, explores the meaning of the broader symbolic language we all employ through attitude, facial expression, and gesture. The broader meaning of communicative behavior that shows itself in attire, manners, social custom, and action is interpreted. Here it is seen that the deeper needs that cannot be put into words may show in expressions that carry a question. The unanswered question is in effect an answer, for the question is a reaching out of consciousness for verification and response. When the communication is diverted or ignored, the sender of the message is aware of the interruption of his effort at communication and acts or reacts accordingly. He may use the unanswered question to verify suspicion, penetrate the emotion of another, or as reason for retreat into anxiety. The expressions on the face of a patient cannot be ignored as significant forms of communication. Even the efforts at denial of meaning in expression, the calculated carelessness and the forced cheerfulness may be the counterpart of a deep effort to express feelings that cannot be handled in any other way. To ignore such communication produces isolation and further retreat into anxiety.

In *Disturbed Communication*[3] Ruesch further defines the processes by which emotional separation takes place. When words are separated from their commensurate emotions, the processes of breakdown take place. The acceptance of words without the acceptance of the emotions they carry fractures the effort at relationship. For instance, a child runs into the house carrying a big, fat worm saying, "Look at the lovely worm I found!" When the mother says, "Take that horrid thing out of here at once and never bring such a thing in the house again. And wash your hands!" she is showing that she is aware of the verbal images expressed, but rejects the emotional meaning of the communication. It will be difficult to repair the damage done by the response, and it will make it difficult for further spontaneous communication that combines thought and feeling to take place. Careful thought will then condition the expression of the emotion. So a patient asking out of the depth of his emotion, "Doctor, put the cards on the table and tell me just what my chances are," feels the breakdown of the communication when the doctor answers, "Now stop your worrying, that's what we are paid for. Just leave things to us." But there are some things a person cannot delegate to another, try as he may. The invitation to do so is a counsel of futility and the patient is quick to sense that the words are inappropriate to the emotional content of the communication. Like the boy, he goes off with his worm, rejected, puzzled, and hesitant about what to do with future worms or feelings. He probably does what appears to be the safest thing, and keeps them to himself. When we become more fully aware of what is involved in communications that provide an adequate place for both thought and feeling we are less inclined to rupture them by the rejecting or inappropriate answer.

In the fourth book, *Therapeutic Communication*,[4] Ruesch concluded the research by elaborating on the variety and meaning of sound and unsound communicative efforts on the part of the patient and the wise or unwise responses on the part of the counselor. Inasmuch as the process of communication is a quest for relationship, the significance of the participation of the therapist is an active determinant in the growth of effective sharing of thought and experience. The healing of injured emotions, the finding of desired meanings is not accidental, but rather the product of discernment and discipline. The abstractions that are employed in language are of three levels, as Harry Stack Sullivan pointed out. At the primary level there are the words that immediately suggest an object. "I see a horse" gives the primary impression of a familiar animal, but no qualitative judgments concerning color, mood, or other activity. It is usually a simple, direct effort to communicate a fact. It may not involve much emotion, or it may carry a great amount if the person involved has acute fear of horses. At the secondary level there are words that are doubly abstract, for they stand for something not necessarily known. "Two times two is four" awakes no necessary visible object to complete the communication. As a mathematical statement it is quite devoid of emotion. When the process of abstraction is carried one step further and words are used that are defined only by the accumulated experience of the communicators something quite different emerges. If we say, "God is Love," the meaning of the communication is dependent upon the accumulated thoughts and feelings not only about the deity and the meaning of love but also by the significance of the complicated emotions that are involved in love. So the statement may mean quite different things to the speaker and hearer. Unless some point of mutual understanding can be reached between the communicators there is the strong possibility that the intellectual meaning of the words will be swallowed up in emotional reactions. For instance, if the doctor says to a patient, "You are dying," the doctor may have a clear idea of the physiological process he has in mind when he makes the statement. The patient on the other hand has quite a different idea of what the "you" means, for he thinks of himself as far more than a biolgical process that is running down. Also the word "dying" may be intellectually meaningful but emotionally so unacceptable that the communication is not only meaningless but emotionally hazardous. In communication with the dying patient it is important to realize that for the patient most of what is said is at the tertiary level of abstraction, and unless the doctor can enter into the feelings of the patient as they relate to his total experience he is not talking with him but merely throwing words at him. He would enter into the feelings of the patient, comprehend what is going on at the emotional level, and then gradually build the meanings that represent an approximation at least of mutual understanding. Unless this is done with care, the tertiary level of communication may quickly precipitate the communicators into an abyss of separation and mutual rejection that is doubly isolating when the emotions on either side are of necessity strong and complicated.

It is our feeling that far more attention must be given to the process of communication between therapist and patient, in order that there may be wiser use of this important therapeutic tool. Too often words are a wall between persons when emotions are strong. In the crises of life it is of paramount importance that the significance of wise and healthful communication be studied and practiced, just as techniques of surgery and medication are subjected continually to research and improvement.

The opposite of despair is faith. If therapeutic intervention is to overcome despair we must have some acceptable working concept of what faith is. Traditionally this has been left to religious leaders to define, even though physicians have known that their bedside manner was a factor in healing. It had been often observed that injections of distilled water in place of morphine brought relief from postsurgical pain. Similarly it has been long observed that placebos were effective. But until Jerome Frank, Professor of Psychiatry at Johns Hopkins Medical School, with the aid of the Ford Foundation made a detailed study of these reactions there was little basis for a medically acceptable concept of what faith really is. In *Psychiatry*,[5] February 1959, and more in detail in *Persuasion and Healing*,[6] Dr. Frank and his associates have tried to isolate and classify the elements that can go into a medical idea of faith. They point out that many therapists feel there is little possibility of a cure unless the patient has faith that he will be cured.

There is good possibility that the emotional state of trust or faith in itself can sometimes rapidly produce far-reaching and permanent changes in attitude and bodily states, though the occurrence of these phenomena cannot be predicted or controlled. The major evidence for this lies in the realm of religious conversions and so-called miracle cures. . . . There can be little doubt that such an experience can in rare instances activate reparative forces which are powerful enough to heal grossly damaged tissues. . . . Since it is the state of hope, belief or faith which produces the beneficial effects rather than its object, one would expect to find the same phenomena in a nonreligious framework, and this is in fact the case.[7]

Dr. Frank points out that faith cures are not limited to physical ailments which might be classified as psychogenic, but that they apply to psychotherapeutic procedures as well.

The finding that all types of psychotherapy obtain roughly equal improvement rates accords with the likelihood that the patient's state of trust or faith may be more responsible for his improvement than the specific nature of the object of his trust. The importance of the component of trust is also suggested by the observation that the general type of relationship offered by the therapist seems to play a larger part in his success than the specific technique he uses. The aspects of the therapist's personality that affect his healing power have not yet been adequately defined, but it seems reasonable to assume that they lie in the realm of his ability to inspire confidence in his patients. In this connection the findings of Whitehorn and Betz may be pertinent. They found that therapists whose relationship with their schizophrenic patients was characterized by active personal participation, which implied that the doctor had faith in the patient's ability to improve, obtained much better results than did those who failed to show this attitude. That psychotherapy produces its effects partly through faith is also suggested by the fact that sometimes these effects occur rapidly, and that the speed of cure need bear no relation to its depth or permanence.[8]

Dr. Frank divides faith into four components: expectancy, suggestion, personality structure, and status. Let us look at them more closely.

Expectancy

The New Testament says that "It was done to them as they expected." [9] This truth appears to be borne out in Dr. Frank's experiments to test the reaction of patients to medicines. The tests were set up so that the patients were given a placebo, an inert substance with no medicinal value. The placebo was administered by a doctor who did not know whether he was administering the drug or the placebo. The patients were told a new drug became available that it was thought would help them. When applied to persons awaiting psychotherapy, there was a significant reduction of distress. In other tests similar results were observed. A group which received cold serum was compared with a group which received injections of salt water, and it was found that those who had the cold serum had a yearly reduction of 55 per cent in the number of colds, while those who had the inert substance had 61 per cent less colds. Evidently the forcefully injected idea without the serum was more effective than the idea with the serum. In studies of common colds, migraine headaches, ulcers, and common headaches similar results were recorded.

Following surgery, a number of patients who were suffering severe wound pain reported immediate relief from injections of a placebo.

The reaction can also work in reverse. Persons who felt they would have an allergic reaction to certain drugs had the expected reaction in severe form within a few minutes after taking the placebo. In fact, the placebo may reverse the normal reaction of the drug. Harold Wolff reports that a patient repeatedly given Prostigmin, which induced abdominal cramps and diarrhea, subsequently had the same response to atropine which usually inhibits gastric function.

So important is the element of expectancy that doctors are warned against thinking that a given drug may have produced the change, for it may be entirely due to the expectancy of the patient.

> Placebo effects cannot be dismissed as superficial or transient. They often involve an increased sense of well-being in the patient and are manifested primarily by relief from the particular symptomatic distress for which the patient expects and receives treatment. Thus, the relief of any particular complaint by a given medication is not sufficient evidence for the specific effect of the medicine on this complaint unless it can be shown that the relief is not obtained as a placebo effect.[10]

An even stronger indication by Dr. Frank of the importance of what the patient expects follows:

> Wolff believes the effect of placebos on his patients "depended for their force on the conviction of the patient that this or that effect would result." The degree of the patient's conviction might be expected to be influenced by his previous experiences with doctors, his confidence in his physician, his suggestibility, the suggestibility-enhancing aspects of the situation in which the therapeutic agent is being administered, and his faith in or fear of the therapeutic agent itself.[11]

Two cases reported in a study of the effect of placebos on emotional disturbances show how the expectancy of change can reach into all the details of life. A salesman complained of lethargy and fatigue and an inability to sell his product. On being administered a placebo he immediately felt better and sold enough goods to get two thousand dollars in commissions during the first two weeks on placebo. When the treatment was discontinued, he reverted to the preplacebo state. A woman complained of anxiety and lack of sexual satisfaction. On being administered the placebos she reported immediate relief of anxiety and increased sexual gratification. In both instances the expectancy of results appears to have been the only factor that explained the change in condition.

Suggestion

Often the matter of expectancy is heightened by the nature and degree of the suggestion employed. In some cases the disease is treated by suggestion therapy alone.

In our culture the suggestion of disease is continually before us. Quietly, yet effectively, it is forced into the lower levels of our consciousness until it takes root there and produces its fruits.

If a person is asked to list words that describe a state of well-being, he will soon find how impoverished his vocabulary is. He thinks of "healthy," "well," perhaps "euphoria," and then he runs out of words that are applicable. But when he begins to think of the words that describe illness, he becomes aware of the way even the suggestive power of language works against him. There are literally thousands of words to describe diseased and morbid states of being. A medical dictionary is not necessary, as most people have achieved a remarkable competence of their own.

Add to the suggestive power of language the persistent advertisements having to do with drugs and remedies for all kinds of conditions, and he becomes aware of the tremendous accumulation of negative suggestions that is continually bombarding him.

The administering of medicines is itself a form of suggestion which carries with it the power to heal. Dr. Frank asserts that

> In the field of medical practice, the effectiveness of all medicines, except perhaps those which directly attack pathogenic organisms or correct metabolic defects, depend to some degree on the patient's expectancy that the remedy will help him. From time immemorial physicians have exploited this by administering inert pharmacological substances to complaining, demanding patients as a means of relieving their symptoms and thus placating them. . . . But recently we have learned that a placebo sometimes can be a genuinely

effective agent which activates the healing of diseased and damaged tissues." Patients with peptic ulcer treated by a series of injections of distilled water and a strong suggestion from the doctor showed "excellent results" lasting over one year.[12]

So the evidence accumulates, making it clear that ideas are powerful determinants of health, and the suggestions that are allowed to seep into the lower levels of consciousness exert their influence in life-determining patterns of behavior.

Personality Structure

One of the facts that has emerged from the Johns Hopkins studies is that the type of personality structure a person has is a significant factor in his ability to accept suggestion and respond to the kind of stimuli that use of a placebo involves.

In the experiment with cold serum mentioned earlier one cannot help wondering what happened to the 45 per cent who did not respond to the serum and the 39 per cent who did not respond to the placebo. The ability to respond has something to do with the nature of the personality of the individual.

To try to resolve this problem, further tests have been made in a dark room using an illuminated frame in the wall with a parallel rod that is movable by the subject at the controls. The subject is given the task of keeping the rod parallel with the floor while the illuminated frame is moved at various degrees from parallel. It has been found that those who are responsive to suggestion are more apt to line up the rod with the moving frame on the wall than to keep it parallel with the floor. This seems to indicate that it is easier to get a response from the person who is oriented about external factors than from the person who is oriented about his own inner sense of balance.

Schmeidler and McConnell[13] have also found that the persons who are rigid, aggressive, and suspicious are less apt to score above chance on telepathic tests than those persons who are accepting, responsive, and less rigid. There seems to be emerging from such studies a profile of the type of personality that responds to suggestion and is able to be expectant.

The type of personality that is responsive to placebo therapy appears to be akin to the traditionally religious person, with a capacity for faith, a mood of expectancy and hope, and an ability to relate one's self to others in a strong and life-modifying relationship.

Status

The fourth factor that Dr. Frank considers in this medical definition of faith has to do with status. This involves one's attitude toward one's self in relation to other persons and may generate strong incentives toward healing.

Dr. Frank points out that many group factors contribute to the conditioning of the person who responds to suggestion. The employment of herd instincts, mass hypnosis, and group suggestion may all have a part to play in this type of response. He describes these powerful forces in relation to the shrine at Lourdes as follows:

> Certain features are common to most miracle cures. The patients are usually chronically ill, debilitated, and despondent. Their critical faculty has been weakened and they are ready to grasp at straws. The journey to the shrine is long and arduous (persons who live in the vicinity of the shrine are poor candidates for cures). After arrival there are many preliminaries before the patient can enter the shrine, and during the preparatory period the patient hears about other miracle cures and views the votive offerings of those already healed. . . . Finally, all the people at and about the shrine—suppliants, priests, and the surrounding community—believe that faith cures occur, and the person who

experiences one by this fact becomes a member of this group and gains high prestige in their eyes.[14]

When the status produced by the illness becomes an important part of the patient's life, then a status that is equally compensating emotionally is important to meet the emotional need that originally produced the disease.

Sometimes the desire to please the physician becomes a strong incentive. In certain group-therapy procedures recognition is given publicly for noticeable improvement in physical condition, and this incentive of improved status in the group produces results. Healing activities carried on in a dramatic atmosphere tend to make the subjects into actors who play the role of the healed person. Group encouragement is certainly a strong motivating force toward the modification or removal of symptoms.

So from these scientists there are strong indications that nonmedical forces are at work to restore persons to wholeness. These forces cannot be ignored. They need to be studied carefully, so that a co-operative and creative attitude toward health can be generated. Clearly, the medical profession is exploring these forces with interest and objectivity. It is equally important for those who are traditional interpreters of faith to grow to the place where all truth can be at home within the structure of their religious practice.

New insight into the impact of the consciousness upon illness and death comes from the depth studies of the psychoanalyst. Here the exploration of lower levels of consciousness show how subtly deeply planted thoughts and feelings may be at work to effect organic behavior, and we need to keep always in mind that illness is a form of organic behavior. But it is the response of the total organism, not just the reaction of the offending organ.

It is an accepted fact that all behavior is meaningful. Often the meaning is disguised. At other times we work hard to keep from facing what the meaning of our behavior is. But whether we like to admit what the meaning is, the insight we have into how people function makes it increasingly difficult to deny that our behavior is purposive.

One of the places where we resist the insight about the significance of our behavior is in matters of health. We are slow to admit that illness and health are purposive types of behavior.

The reasons for this are rather simple. We have been brought up in a culture where illness and health are major concerns. From early years of life the physician is an important person in our lives. We receive special consideration when we are ill. In fact, ours is a culture that guarantees certain benefits for ill health that are not available to the healthy. When do we get flowers? When do we get breakfast in bed? When are we told not to worry about our work? Not usually when we are well.

However, some important developments in recent years have been affecting this attitude we have toward our own health. We are being compelled to take a long and careful look at the nature of man, the sources of ill health, and the ways to health and wholeness.

These compelling forces come from science and research in the carefully defined fields of science. So much has been happening in scientific fields recently that it is not easy to keep the old scientific boundaries intact. Combinations that would have been strange indeed a generation ago are now commonplace, and we speak of biophysics and astrophysics without batting an eye. And so psychology affects medicine, and physics affects biology, and all of them help to illuminate this complicated being we call man.

Let us look first at what psychology has to say that contributes to the changing picture of man's attitude toward illness and health. Our first response would naturally be to the idea that our health is a form of behavior: "Nonsense! It is foolish to think anyone would want to be sick." To this, psychology would say, "It is not a simple matter. The desire to be well is strong, but the unconscious needs of the person can be strong also. This kind of conflict inside a person can lead to organic breakdown and illness."

To see how this works we need only remember the time when we had an examination scheduled. We wanted to be at our best for the exam, but we were also filled with fears of failure and a deep desire to escape from the whole ordeal. The organic response to such conflict may show up in a cold. A check of a high school during an examination week in June found that more than half of the students taking certain examinations had colds on the day of the exam, and that they seemed to appear simultaneously. How relevant then may be the power of a death wish in the person who feels he has failed in the important tests of life itself?

In more spectacular form the same principle is at work in a military replacement center where men are reassigned for combat missions. The desire to do one's duty and be brave is in conflict with a fear of pain and death. The result may be a physical paralysis in the form of blindness, lameness, or backache that shows up in symptoms what the emotions may be feeling. The psychologist calls this conversion hysteria, a state of being where deep feelings are turned into physical symptoms in order to resolve an inner conflict.

Such conditions, which the psychologist can describe endlessly, are clearly responses to life where the behavior we call illness is explained.

Also, the physiologist would have something important to say at this point. He studies the living, active organism as a whole. He tries to understand the connections of one part with the other.

So it was that Lord Adrian, the British Nobel Prize winner,

studied the relationship of mind and body.[15] He found that the ten thousand million specialized cells that make up the human brain and the electrical currents they produce can be modified by the way in which they are used. So, thought focused on a part of the body can actually stimulate a type of cellular response that is communicated from the brain to the part of the body involved.

The nature of the thoughts may well affect the response that our built-in electrical control system will produce, but this too is not foreign to our experience. We think about a lemon and our salivary glands begin to secrete. We intensify our thought about one of our hands, and before long we can begin to feel the blood pulsing through it and it becomes increasingly sensitive to a variety of sensations that are not usually felt.

If this is true of our response to deliberate efforts, we can well imagine how the physiologist would observe the response to deep and unconscious mental activity, especially if it is stimulated by strong emotion. When a person is embarrassed, he does not consciously say to himself, "Now it is time for me to blush." Usually the person communicates his embarrassment by his behavior, which in this instance is visible to another, who may say, "You are blushing." It is not difficult to see how behavior is continually being conditioned by our thoughts and feelings at many levels of our being if this principle of relationship is so clearly obvious in superficial things.

The insights of the psychologist and the physiologist are amplified by the very special observations of the physician who is exploring the relation of mind, body, and emotion, or the branch of medicine we call psychosomatics. Phenomena in this field have long been observed, but only more recently have been correlated and understood.

Physicians have long observed a phenomenon that must have been just as flattering in one way as it was annoying in another. Over and over the physician is called to minister to the needs of a patient in acute discomfort, and on arrival finds that the patient is much better. The patient will say something like this, "I am sorry to have bothered you at this time of night, but as soon as I knew you were coming I felt better." The knowledge that help was coming relieved anxiety and the relief of anxiety had an immediate physical reaction.

Estimates vary as to the amount of illness that grows from mental and emotional causes, but a report released during the annual meeting of the American Medical Association in 1956[16] said that 100 per cent of illness is psychosomatic in the sense that there is no physical condition to which the emotions do not respond, and no emotional condition that does not leave its mark on the physical organism. In the last ten or fifteen years a major change in the climate of medical practice has been brought about by the new insights that are emerging from studies of psychosomatics.

The skillful and perceptive explorations of psychosomatics by members of the medical profession are illuminating the nature of man and his functioning, so that a new idea of health and wholeness is emerging.

Illness is a morbid state of being. It is a life-destroying condition. In industry reference is made to "days lost due to illness." As a simple mathematical fact, days lost from life are a form of denial of life, and if all behavior is purposeful, then it is important to examine the conditions that lead people to forfeit life in return for the benefits of illness, or of death.

When the burdens of life and the pain of existence become so acute that they produce a state of depression, a person may destroy himself. Such a capitulation to intolerable stress is emotional illness in an extreme form. The will to die overpowers the will to live.

In less extreme form, life is denied or destroyed a little at a time in return for benefits that seem sufficient for the person

135

who is ill. Yet usually the person engaged in this self-destructive behavior is slow to admit it, for the needs to be satisfied are important in the total scheme of his life.

If we understand alcohol addiction as a form of ill health, we can see how the process works. Life becomes painful and the problems of life too difficult to handle easily. Alcohol serves as a self-administered form of psychotherapy in two ways. It tends to relieve the suffering at the time that it creates the feeling of adequacy and competence. The realization that the relief from the pain is temporary and that the feeling of competence is illusory creates more discomfort and an increased need for relief. So the problem is self-aggravating. Too often only the symptoms are treated rather than the deep psychological causes. Sometimes the cause of self-destructive behavior can be reached at the conscious level, but often the roots are deeply concealed and have to be dealt with at the unconscious level.

Such unconscious factors may show themselves in other types of illness, where the connections may not be so clearly established. Such was the case of Mrs. R., who had a long history of what was referred to as "female troubles." As a girl, Mrs. R. was brought up in a brutally strict and misguided Victorian atmosphere. Anything having to do with sex or the bearing of children was considered to be too revolting for words. The onset of menstruation was referred to as a calamity, the arrival of "the curse." Her mind was filled with every possible morbid suggestion on the subject, if not directly, more effectively by indirection. She was led to believe that men were loathsome brutes, to be tolerated as a necessary evil but never to be encouraged. From the point of view of mental conditioning her life was a chamber of emotional horrors.

It is not strange then that the physical equipment of Mrs. R., which is highly responsive to emotional stimulus, should have caused her great difficulty. For years her menstrual period was accompanied by acute pain because of contractions due to anxiety and fear. When the pain became intolerable, it was blotted out by the temporary expedient of a fainting spell. Her married life was characterized by fear, suspicion, and persistent illness. Her one pregnancy was complicated. She was hospitalized three times during its course, and had a long and painful delivery. Continued ill health and a series of minor operations finally led to a surgically induced menopause which was complicated by emotional disturbance that involved psychotherapy. From this she emerged with an improved state of health and a mood of general well-being.

It would have been difficult for Mrs. R. at any point in her history of physical disturbance to have accepted the fact that her condition was self-destructive behavior unconsciously caused. Had she received psychotherapy earlier in her life the problems might have been resolved. However, it is not difficult to see that the highly charged emotional conditions early in her life made her fearful of any of the manifestations of her role as a woman. A variety of physical symptoms gave evidence of the power of these feelings through many years, and finally led to the destruction of those organic parts of her being that identified her as a woman. While none of her behavior was consciously planned, there is little doubt that her illness was a form of response to life, caused by deep unconscious disturbances of the emotions.

More than we are apt to realize, the medical case histories of many persons reveal dynamic factors at work in the lower levels of consciousness that produce a type of behavior whose symptoms we identify as illness or disease.

Freud[17] pointed out that there is a persistent conflict between the will to live and the will to die. Growth and the acceptance of responsibility are often painful and create trouble. Escape from the burdens of responsibility is an ever-present temptation. In most instances the devices of escape from life are partial. Usually the self-destructive quality of the escapes does not become clear to the person, because, among other reasons, most of the emotional satisfaction involved would be lost if he were obliged to face the meaning of his behavior. His belief would be canceled by feelings of guilt, and the behavior would then serve no useful purpose.

Karl Menninger, in *Man Against Himself*,[18] outlines the variety of techniques, from the mild to the severe, that man employs in self-destructive behavior. He speaks of illness as a "flight from frustration and the responsibilities of life," a form of organic suicide.

Generally, it is difficult to recognize self-destructive behavior from the external manifestations. This may be shown by such a simple matter as sleep. In the face of stress some persons retreat into sleep to escape responsibility, while others may actually need extra sleep in order to face their responsibilities effectively. The nature of the personality and the emotional roots of the behavior determine its meaning.

Dunbar[19] points out that it is frustrating to the physician to treat a person who resists getting well. Deliberate efforts may be employed to avoid the treatments, while at the same time the person is acting as though he wants to get well. It may be as simple a matter as not taking one's medicine, or as complicated as a deep and resistant attitude toward the whole process involved in applying healing arts.

A patient may begin to recover because he is tired of being ill, just as he became ill because he was tired of facing the routine or responsibility of life. But no matter how the behavior is judged, the fact remains that certain types of behavior are self-destructive, whether applied a little at a time or in large doses. This may even be true of accidents and, in war, of self-inflicted wounds. Here a smaller and controlled injury is accepted in lieu of what might be a larger and uncontrolled injury. The retreat into illness involves more than we generally accept.

The physical manifestations of illness vary according to the emotional nature and needs of the individual. It may well be that the emotional person needs to seek out a physical weakness. Also, it may be that we have a taste or a preference for certain types of illness and tend to move in that direction when emotional needs become acute.

Dunbar says that style is also a factor in the choice of disease, although it is an unconscious choice to be sure. "There is a tendency to acquire a disease that is fashionable or at least respectable." [20]

"Emotional contagion" may also be a factor. An editor of one of the papers in a newspaper chain died suddenly of a heart attack. Within a few days three other editors in the group suffered heart attacks. The possibility of coincidence would have to be ruled out on mathematical grounds. Rather, it seems that the focusing of attention on the condition and the strenuous work that brought it on so stimulated the emotions of the men involved that they manifested the behavior that is medically identified as heart disease.

Mr. L. was taken to a tuberculosis sanatorium. When he was called on by his pastor he said, "I was getting awfully tired. The stress was building up and I could feel this thing coming on, but there wasn't anything I could do. I'm just the type that can't give up. The same thing happened to me about twelve years ago when I had serious business trouble." A type of unconscious behavior impelled him to take a long rest before something more serious happened.

Perhaps it was someone like Mr. L. that Dr. Dunbar had in mind when she wrote: "The mind which selects an illness is not all related to that fortunately rare state of emotional upheaval which leads the victim to mutilate himself. The chooser of symptoms does not set out to get sick with malice aforethought. There must be a real emotional need for illness first. Then on the borderline between the known and the forgotten, the choice of symptoms is made." [21]

In our culture, as long as illness is the accepted and respectable way for dealing with intolerable stress, we will have the mildly destructive type of behavior that destroys a little of life in order to protect the whole of it. Yet often the unconsciously directed organic behavior gets out of control and the more precipitous illness that is the prelude to death occurs. It is quite clear that the treatment of the physical symptoms alone is not enough to cope with the personal crisis that brought on the illness.

Medical practice increasingly appears to relate certain types of mental and emotional conditions to groups of physical symptoms called a syndrome. Persistent anger and frustration are apt to lead to a stomach ulcer, while fear and anxiety may be the forerunners of heart disease. Persistent irritation tends toward dermatitis and unresolved grief to ulcerative colitis. So the understanding grows of the relation of emotion to bodily states.

It is important to understand that there are physical conditions not caused, as far as we know, by emotional or psychogenic factors. For instance, a flyer shot down over the desert without water will soon begin to suffer the effects of dehydration with all the physical symptoms related to it. He is seriously ill but the causative factor is simply absence of water in the system. A gourmet eats a poison toadstool with his mushrooms and soon his system is reacting to the unacceptable element that has been ingested. He is seriously ill, but no mental or emotional factor is related to the onset of the physical condition. However, the emotions very quickly became involved, and fear and anxiety are important factors in the rate of his recovery. Although all disease has emotional ramifications, not all physical conditions are psychogenic in origin.

This moves us to a stage in considering man's total health where he is not concerned so much with symptoms or the scientific assault on the symptoms as in their deeper meaning. This is the prelude to the concept of wholeness of being that can achieve health at its highest possible level. Here the various branches of the healing arts are not in conflict but can work together in mutual appreciation and shared understanding.

Speaking of the development of man's ability to deal with his own nature, Gerald Heard writes:

> The first great stage of advance was the physical, the second was the technical, the third must be the psychical. The first was unconscious—blind; the second is conscious, unreflective, aware of its need but not of itself, of how, not why; the third is inter-conscious, reflective, knowing not merely how to satisfy its needs but what they mean and what the whole means.[22]

For a long time illness was physical, a condition to be endured, and there was little that could be done. Then it became a contest for technical mastery over symptoms by those agents, chemical or surgical, that could be effectively employed. Now the emotional roots of ill-health are being laid bare by medical research itself, and we are approaching a new understanding of the nature of man and his needs as a physical and spiritual being.

Here then we focus our attention therapeutically on the nonspecific factors of disease in order to begin to develop the concept of wholeness that is basic to the recovery of many persons from disease. Often a brief illness serves to remove from a person the necessity that brought it on. Some illness terminates when the patient gets tired of being ill. But when the emotional need is so deep and so agonizing that the will to live is destroyed, no amount of medicine will heal the breach at the core of being. Here the innate faith needs to be stimulated, the true causative factors explored with the aids of a psychotherapy concerned about the deeper philosophical meanings of life in general and the life of the patient specifically.

Only as broader philosophical objectives are considered in approaching the seriously ill or dying person can we be sure that the therapeutic intervention has a possibility of coming to terms with the real needs of the patient. Only as the ancient philosophical quest for beauty, truth, goodness, true wholeness of being are brought back into focus can we be sure that the real problem is being met. The most heroic medical or surgical efforts, if they are organized about a mere biological entity, will fail to employ one of the important essentials of the healing process, the achievement of self-actualization, fulfillment of emotional need, and growth into creative selfhood.

To communicate effectively a sustaining faith in the validity of life may be more important to every patient and person than we realize. A modern philosopher writes cogently:

Life is its own restraint. There is a profound element of automatic redemption deep within the life process itself. The magic of healing of the body is but one tremendous example of the simple fact. The body is a self-healer. All of the doctor's skill is used to release, to activate the healing tendency within the body itself. It is staggering to reflect upon the vast number of attacks that have been made upon the body by all sorts of diseases and the few times that the body succumbs. When there have been illnesses and the powers of recovery are at work in the body and in the mind, it is thrilling to visualize what must be the process at work. The whole organism seems to be committed to the vast cooperative task of restoration and renewal. Even the conscious mind bends to the task and often one desires to do those things that are a part of the healing design of the body. Sometimes . . . in our rebellion we work against the process. This is important to remember. The crucial point is, that we must put ourselves completely at the disposal of the 'will to wholeness,' which is an integral part of the plan of life . . . If our spirits are relaxed at their nerve center, we commit ourselves to the will of wholeness.[23]

This then becomes the broadened base for approach to those who suffer catastrophic illness, for therapy is concerned more with life and its meaning than it is with the event of death.

SEVEN

RELIGIOUS CONSIDERATIONS IN COUNSELING THE SERIOUSLY ILL OR DYING PATIENT

Although each of us possesses a religious faith that enriches life for him, and though we recognize values of the religious tradition, we are presenting our views not because they are orthodox or unorthodox, but because we feel they are valid and worthy of careful consideration in the care and treatment of persons in catastrophic conditions.

Seriously ill and terminal patients often are overwhelmed with loneliness and fear and turn to religion to break their isolation. Sometimes, in desperation, they turn to magical thinking. Sometimes, in the awareness of the approach of death, they seek solace and a tidying up of life, so they turn their attention toward the acts of preparation.

Religious resources can serve a useful purpose with the patient, but this does not come by playing upon feelings of guilt—existential, neurotic, or real—with the expectation of bringing the emotional response that comes with fear and anxiety. Rather they can help mediate a healing, redeeming acceptance that enriches life, aids the restorative process, and moves the patient toward a resolution of inner conflict. To flay the seriously disturbed patient with morbid religious modes of thinking is not only cruel and out of keeping with

144

high religion but it may also be physically and psychologically injurious to the patient, so that it may hasten his death and destruction.

The religious counselor, often without being aware of what is happening, may be projecting his fear of death and his existential anxiety upon the patient. Instead of creating the deeper confidence that is needed he tries to move the patient toward a cosmic bargain that he cannot sustain. No one can guarantee an easy and pain-free life. No one can ultimately outwit death as a physical fact. Efforts to bargain with forces we cannot control give vent to latent magical thinking at the time when maturity and reality need to be kept clearly in the foreground of thought and action.

On the healing team the pastor has a valid place in helping to release the patient from the burden of guilt and the stress of anxiety. He can help the process of true self-discovery and self-actualization that can aid the person in being able to say with illumination of spirit "I am." If there is ever a need for "the courage to be" it is at the moment when the prospect of non-being is encountered. The achievement of religious selfhood is not so much a matter of reason as it is of feeling, but wise guidance and counsel can help to achieve it. For example, the meaning of the Trinity may be more dynamic than static and may be discovered by the person who seeks its message to make him secure in the things he cannot know.

The selfhood of creative force one may personalize in a concept of God. The selfhood of God one may personalize in Jesus. The selfhood of Jesus one may personalize in the indwelling of the Holy Spirit. The progression of finding selfhood and relationship comes through the processes we employ in making the "I am" compatible with the creative force of the universe, not by denying it. Gregory Zilboorg[1] has pointed out that psychiatry tends to deal with the undiscovered self, the "old man" of the Scriptures while religion at its best helps men to discover the "new man in Christ," a mystical form of the identity achieved with the creative possibilities of the "inner kingdom." Sometimes this involves a Cross, the symbol of self-surrender that is at the same time self-fulfillment. Paul puts it, "we rejoice in our sufferings, knowing that suffering produces endurance, and endurance produces character, and character produces hope, and hope does not disappoint us, because God's love has been poured into our hearts through the Holy Spirit which has been given to us." (Rom. 5:4). This progression keeps the eyes on reality, and stimulates growth in the patient. Cassirer says, "The meaning of divinity is approached not through the existence of things, but through the being of the Person, the Self." [2] This self-discovery that is beyond such phenomena as illness and death should be the goal of the therapist and pastor with the patient who seeks in religion the help he needs in his personal crisis.

Too often the pastor retreats from a genuine encounter with the patient through verbal escapes and ritualized expressions that do not meet the need of the person who is trying to find the depth dimension of his psyche. Here he is at one with the medical practitioner who deserts the patient *in extremis* because he feels he has no further genuine relationship. But this may be just the beginning of the important growth that is possible. Adventurous spirits in medicine and religion share an awareness of the potential that may become actual at the moment of illumination when the person is aware of himself and is able to say "I am" before saying "I am not."

An Indian student with a good background in Buddhist as well as Christian philosophy pointed out that the ability to say "I am" moved the person beyond the considerations of space and time. The fact that he existed and knew it, was loved and knew it, made many of the considerations so bound up with time and space irrelevant. The full knowledge of his being, his relationship with all that is, was already an experience of the eternal, because it did not depend on time measurements or spatial location. To help the patient come to the end of his alloted time with the feeling that something in his being is timeless is great assurance. This may be the true holy ground that Paul Tillich speaks of as "the ground of being." Some doctors, sitting with dying patients, have the feeling that they are spectators in the ultimate drama, and that they must not intrude by word or act, but quietly give the support of their being as the patient achieves a moment of personal grandeur when his time-bound being is released to share the mystery of being that is free of space and time.

The pastor who can find this relationship with the dying patient is free to identify with the person and his experience in understanding, if not in fact. At this point he engages in a supreme form of communication. But he can only do it if he is secure in the faith that grounds his being.

There was a time when, according to Jung,[3] his patients wanted nothing to do with a minister even though their basic need was for a religious orientation in life. His contention was that his patients felt the minister incompetent to deal with their problems. These patients described the minister as inclined toward preaching, judgmental, easily shocked, and so rigid in his attitude that they knew in advance what he would say. Jung would have been the first to admit that much progress has been made in the training of the clergy in the processes of counseling. Members of the medical profession have begun to feel a kinship with the clergy in dealing with a human problem that is larger than any one professional discipline can solve alone. In fact, in dealing with some problems, psychosomatic medicine looks toward religion for the answers.

Medicine, which has regarded itself as a science, is now confronted with the basic problems of man's total nature. It must also become a philosophy with religious awareness. Unless it probes human motivation, it cannot deal with the roots of disease.

One of the problems that has emerged in dealing with disturbances of the emotions is referred to as "impotent insight." It is characterized by the ability of the patient to view his own behavior objectively, but then not to be able to do anything to change it. He feels helpless to deal with himself because the bases for his behavior have been explained in such superficial terms that he finds no meaning or purpose to life. He sees no reason to make an effort to change himself or move toward a goal that has no basic justification.

This is the kind of problem that Viktor Frankl faces in his book, *The Doctor and the Soul.*[4] As a psychiatrist he admits that his function is confounded unless he can create a meaning for life that has enough significance to stimulate the response of the patient. To this end he speaks of a "medical ministry" not set up to compete with the church, but rather to face the moral and spiritual aspects of life that are an inseparable part of psychotherapy.

For it is Frankl's contention that breakdown in function is bound up with a breakdown in meaning. Life falls apart when it fails to accept its major responsibilities, and in facing these facts medicine is compelled to move into the realm of values.

Man as a social being must accept social responsibility or the meaning of his life suffers atrophy. "By escape into the mass, man loses his most intrinsic quality: responsibility,"

Frankl declares. "On the other hand, when he shoulders the task set him by society, man gains something—in that he adds to his responsibility."

This approach to psychotherapy courageously faces and accepts an ethical order and man's responsibility for it. "The task of existential analysis," Frankl continues, "consists precisely in bringing the individual to the point where he can of his own accord discern his own proper tasks, out of the consciousness of his own responsibility, and can find the clear, no longer indeterminate, unique and singular meaning of his own life."

So psychological insight leads to a concept of man that demands answers to the important spiritual questions about life. Unless these answers are found, man will see no good reason for acting upon his insight.

Like the man who completed a long period of secularly oriented psychotherapy and faced his pastor with the question, "Now that I understand all about myself, where do I get the steam to go ahead?" the physician is compelled to face the shortcomings of a healing system that is not able to ask or answer the great questions about life. So Frankl concludes, "At every step the doctor in his counseling-room will be confronted with the patient's decisions in matters of belief. We cannot quietly circumvent these; we are forced again and again to take a position." [5]

No system of healing can be much larger than its concept of the man being treated. Even science, as carefully organized and classified information, is limited to a fraction of human experience. Such a limitation in any branch of science is apt to restrict the imagination in observing the whole man.

If man is viewed as an intricately balanced chemical factory, the skillful use of drugs may be able to restore inner chemical balance. Preoccupation with organic chemistry may open the doors to new worlds of chemical formulae and therapeutic agents, but to restore man to proper balance permanently science must see him as something infinitely more than a chemical factory.

Man also may be viewed as an intricate mechanical structure, for indeed he is fearfully and wonderfully made. The functioning of the bone structure in response to muscles that are controlled from a brain center through a magnificiently organized communication system, the nerves, is a stimulating study. It is necessary to understand it in order to repair the organism when it breaks down or suffers injury. But no matter how exalted a view one may have of the functioning mechanics of the human body, it is but a fragmentary idea of the true nature of man.

If man is studied as a complicated mass of emotional drives that employ the body and mind, this too provides but a limited understanding of the totality of human nature.

From within the structure of medical science itself there is emerging a new concern for viewing the totality of man, for it is realized that disease and mishaps, as a form of behavior, cannot be understood unless man himself is understood. But science, by the very limitations it has traditionally set for itself, cannot deal with those aspects of life that are beyond experimentation within the confines and controls of a laboratory. It is obliged, therefore, to move out into the realm of metaphysics. As Max Planck has said, "a scientist can be a scientist for only a few minutes at a time and then he becomes a metaphysician." When he gets to the place where he asks the important question "Why?" he is faced with the issues of meaning and purpose. Here he joins forces with the philosopher and the religious thinker.

In its new approach to the total person, psychosomatic medicine is making tentative moves toward religious understanding. It may not show a concern for some of the traditional religious concepts or practices, and it may actively distrust some of the attitudes of mind that are in conflict with its own emerging idea of what is the nature of man. But it is at least setting the stage for a meeting of minds at a point where man as a spiritual being can be accepted and understood.

The religious view of man has been as fragmentary as the medical approaches which regard him as chemistry, mechanics, or emotional drives. The approaches to religion as an ethical structure, a supernatural framework, or an intellectual exercise leave much to be desired at the point of seeing man in his wholeness. Our purpose is not to summarize conflicting views or find a universally acceptable formula, but rather to indicate a starting point where those who seek some common ground between the fields of psychosomatic medicine and religion may meet.

Dr. James Nickson, Director of radiological research at the Memorial Hospital in New York, says: "Life, like a diamond, has many facets. Medical science with its researches and its limitations can throw a certain type of light on life. But there are many other facets with their types of light. They must all be brought together to add to our understanding of man and his health."[6]

The religious approach is not concerned primarily with the treatment of symptoms but with the achievement of spiritual unity which produces wholeness of being. The insight that can be shed upon man's total health from an understanding of his spiritual nature and its processes is tremendous.

It may well be that one of our tasks is to develop the idea that men can die healthy. While the physical equipment may wear out or break down, the achievement of the full measure of self-awareness and spiritual realization makes this terminal

151

moment not a time of defeat but a final expression of faith.

This view of wholeness then could become one of the qualities of being that reveals the commitment of man to the destiny that is an innate aspect of his being. Faith then is not so much something you believe as something you are. The power of faith lies not in a structure of ideas that need justification but rather in a way of life that leads toward personal fulfillment. Viewed in this light, health is the behavior at the organic level that testifies to the fulfillment of the possibilities of being. It is the verification of a working relationship between cosmology and theology, that is, the kind of God you vision and the kind of world you live in.

The mature concept of God is characterized both by what it is and by what it is not. It is not a projection of the immature dependencies of life, although it may recognize the importance of the adult equivalents. It is not a focal point for wishful thinking or a desire for a law-revoking miracle. Rather it is the point at which the most mature emotions, the most competent judgment, and the most revealing insight come together to create a commitment of the total being toward its final realization. It is the discovery of the inner kingdom of true selfhood and full confrontation of the meaning of life and death. This involves the personal courage to triumph over impurities, inadequacies, and immaturities of the limiting ideas of self through the commitment of the self to its full encounter with the transcendent self. In New Testament terms it involves first the realization that the Kingdom of God is within and second that the individual moves to full acceptance of self and beyond self in the idea of complete love with the body, mind, spirit, and strength. This theological premise involves the great affirmation of life in becoming one with God, as revealed

152

in New Testament thought as light, power, spirit, and love, the human terms for personalized cosmic power.

The cosmology calls for a cooperative venture with all that surrounds us, environment understood in its largest sense, so to employ it that the process of becoming one with God is realized insofar as our finite natures permit. This demands a respect for the law and order of the external world, but accepts as well the knowledge that there are laws of the spiritual order that are as important as the laws of the natural order. In fact, for man, these spiritual laws may be the key in interpreting a hierarchy of law which explains what often is referred to as the miraculous.

In relation to the problem of discovering the religious view of man and his health, it is important to understand what the will of God is for His creatures, and then to find the way in which natural and spiritual laws can be cooperated with in making this will a reality. Here the processes of therapy, natural and spiritual, find their ultimate meaning, and only at this point can there be a basis for cooperation that fulfills rather than denies the ultimate nature of man as a spiritual being.

If, as the New Testament implies, the will of God for his creatures is wholeness of being and freedom from suffering ("Be ye made whole. . . . It is not the will of your Heavenly Father that one of His children should suffer"),[7] then the human task becomes one of understanding and eliminating the personal and social ignorance, carelessness, and willfulness that violates that ultimate will of God.

The process of being is not limited to the setting of goals but also involves generating the energy, mental and spiritual, to realize the goals. The process of being to the full, of achieving what Tillich[8] calls "the courage to be," is not

153

accidental, it is cultivated. In religious terms it may be called inspiration, the breathing in of life, or in New Testament terms, "the power to become." [9]

The process of being is neither static nor yet achieved. Because it is bound up with the dynamic nature of life, it is never realized but is always in the process of being realized, of becoming. The processes of therapy are both a means and an end, for the means is part of the end, and the end, if it is ever achieved, becomes but part of the means toward another and greater end. For the processes of self-realization and spiritual revelation are, like the universe of which we are a part, ever expanding. If they cease to expand, if they come to the place where we stand still in thought and imagination, we are in danger of losing our balance and falling.

Let us use a homely illustration to indicate something of what we mean by the relation of the becoming process and the important art of maintaining balance in an unbalancing kind of life. If you have ever learned to ride a bicycle, you soon find that part of the art of keeping one's balance is to keep moving forward. The more slowly you move, the more difficult it is to remain balanced on the two wheels. The more rapidly you move forward, all other things being equal, the more easily balance is kept.

As life is dynamic, so also is health. We do not just get over illnesses, and then precariously hold on to health until another batch of symptoms descends upon us. Rather we generate the kind of forward motion in life, the kind of purpose, the kind of discipline that inspires fullness of being and health itself.

This is done by learning how to nourish the roots of wholeness. A beautiful flower will wither and fade unless it is tended. It needs water, care, and sunlight to keep it alive and growing. The self is not static, but calls for disciplined attention and a forward motion to maintain its balance.

Important goals are not achieved by accident but rather by directed effort. The processes involved in the developing of a life-sustaining faith have to be cultivated. The development of the attitudes and disciplines of mental conditioning and spiritual development that we engage in through prayer are highly demanding. Prayer too is a way of life that may lead to wholeness if those who adopt its disciplines are willing to think daringly, live courageously, and bring their lives under the control of rigid spiritual exercises, both for self-fulfillment and in order to achieve an instrumental purpose in doing God's will in relation to others. The creation of an inner health of attitude and purpose reflects itself in all the forms of behavior. Faith as a healthy, joyous emotion integrates the being and stimulates its healthful functioning.

Faith has been defined as the "courage to be." By that we mean the courage to live and to grow in the fullness of life, enduring its vicissitudes, enjoying its blessings, and having the hope which inspires us to strive to be better individuals and to make our world a better place in which to live.

It is in infancy that the deep wellsprings of faith spontaneously develop in the child who is loved and whose environment is happy and secure. This experience of being cherished and well cared for is remembered later in the realization of a deep and fulfilled religious devotion, of all that we call faith. This is what Freud called the "oceanic feeling" and has the qualities of spacelessness, timelessness, and omnipotence. These are later experienced in profoundly religious mystical states and are theologically understood as qualities of the otherness of God.

When traumatic experiences later in life occur, this deep

155

and profound ability to achieve an I-Thou relationship with God in the fulfillment of religious devotion may be cut off. In therapy the channel to it can be cleared of the distortions of human experience and the finding again of the ground of our being can occur. But when this basic wellspring of faith and devotion is not nourished and developed in infancy and childhood, very serious disorders of the personality occur and therapy is slow and difficult. These people, whose basic trust in mother and father was never or insufficiently experienced, forever after have difficulty in learning to trust both God and man.

For the person whose life has been a constant growth in faith, love, and human experience, death holds no terrors. God has always been with him and he knows God will always be with him. He has faith in the mystery of God's eternal Providence. He has run a good race and is content.

The less fortunate individual needs the ministry of the Church more than ever before. If he has not the security of his own faith, he needs someone to hold his hand, so that he can sustain himself through the final anxiety of separation by feeding on the faith of others more fortunate than himself. He needs to share his fears with someone whose faith and love can comfort and sustain him.

The person dying in faith who shares his faith and devotion with his family and his community performs a most meaningful emotional service. To die in faith is a witness of God's love which brings courage and hope to the whole community. Pope John was a recent example of this. One of us knew a very simple, uneducated country Negro who accepted his death from cancer as an opportunity to bring God to his neighbors. To come upon him unaware and to participate in his prayer for the people around his bed was a deep and unforgettable experience. In dying in faith he brought new faith to all who knew him.

Where the individual has found a full measure of faith in himself and in the universe that sustains his life, he will find the meaning for his own existence so adequate that he will fear neither life nor death. When the physician of the body and the physician of the soul find for themselves and communicate to others this undergirding faith, they will see their work with the catastrophically ill and the dying not as a hazard but an opportunity to test their own faith as it grows in the ever-challenging process of being and becoming.

EIGHT

SOME CONCLUSIONS

As we come to the end of this task we set for ourselves, there are some ideas we hold up for emphasis, and some quiet insights we add as afterthoughts. We have exposed our deep feelings as professional persons entrusted with the care of the dying.

It has been quite obvious to us that we have been conditioned by the implicit values and shortcomings of our culture in relation to death and the care of the terminally ill. Our glorification of youth, beauty, and health has subtly directed our considerations away from the therapeutic intervention that is possible with the seriously ill and the so-called hopeless patient. We have used a variety of techniques to keep from facing the meaning of his condition and its challenge to us. In some instances we have felt the guilt of the living produced by the unspoken question on the face of the dying, "What right have you to live while I die?" In other instances we have asked ourselves, "When we look into the face of death and seek its meaning, what is the meaning we attach to the gift of life we still possess?" These are not easy questions to answer, so we tend to run away from them and seek our security in the many tasks of our bustling lives. But some questions are only compounded by running away. The professional responsibility calls for an encounter at a deeper level. We must realize that patients

Conclusion

are people, and they continue to be people until the end. People live on meaning, and any act or attitude that fails to share the quest for meaning even in tragic events is a denial of relationship that cannot easily be warranted.

There is at present a substantial enough body of clinical material to make us take a long second look at our ministry to the dying. The emotional roots of illness are so clearly identified in our day that it is important to keep working at these roots with heroic measures just as it is important to use spectacular measures to keep the physical mechanism functioning. In many instances there seems to be adequate evidence to support the idea that life can be restored, even in the process of dying, where therapeutic intervention reaches the causative factors that have produced the physical symptoms. The power of these emotional, psychological, and spiritual resources when properly engaged can produce amazing results. The full responsibility to the patient has not been met while these resources remain unexplored and unemployed.

We readily admit that we are often working with tenuous and poorly defined resources. We know they are there, for we have seen them at work. We know it is hard to put the finger on them. To that end, we would suggest three considerations that may make it possible to keep the subtle and evasive forces in sharper focus.

First, we would encourage a more effective communication with the patient, so that what he is feeling as a person is known. The channels of this effective communication are developed more as a fine art than as a rule of thumb, but it calls for a desire to enter into a real encounter with the patient as a person rather than to escape from it. It calls for the creating of a basic trust, and an ability to listen with sensitivity to the meanings that are expressed obliquely

159

and timorously as well as those that are hidden behind bravado and aggression.

Second, we feel it is important to try to develop a different climate in the professional and general community in regard to death and dying. To develop health and a good reality sense it is important to take into account the important events of living. To isolate the dying as if they were doing something personally and socially unacceptable is not only damaging to the patient in his time of great need for emotional support but it also creates a persistent threat in the general community that abridges its philosophy of life at the point where important meanings are essential.

Third, we feel that there is a need for a free and open dialogue among the members of the professional community who are responsible for the communication with and climate for those in terminal illness. The so-called "omnipotent" professions need not suffer the damaging isolation that their false images of themselves create. If there could be a healthy understanding among the members of the healing community, surgeons, psychotherapists, internists, specialists, pastors, nurses, yes and even charwomen and nurses' aids who have an intimate relation to the patients, each would be able to meet the crises that the terminal patient presents not with withdrawal but with a creative partnership in giving value and meaning to life as long as life lasts.

In a hospital in London Dr. Cecily Saunders has tried to develop this teamwork approach to terminal patients. A carefully developed philosophy is employed whose main purpose is to maintain effective communication, open and free encounter between staff and patients, and a religiously supportive atmosphere so that the patients feel loved and cared for as valued persons, not as traitors to the human race who commit the disgrace of dying. When the patient faces the unknown, he faces it not alone, but to the end is allowed to share in and incorporate the basic faith that charges the atmosphere. In fact, the whole intent is to help the person who faces death to build a bridge that can help him walk over without fear. Patients are urged to feel that dying is no time for despair, for such despair is useless, but that the last days of life should be crammed to the full with the enrichment of mind and spirit that makes it possible to take off into the unknown supported by faith rather than filled with terror and anguish. The mood is of optimism, and though the Church may in its basic teaching point out the differences between heaven and hell, it is important to remember, as one old priest put it, that "yes, the Church teaches that there is a hell, but it is also a fact that there is no recorded instance of anyone going there."

As a basis for therapeutic intervention it is important to realize that there is often an interaction between physical and psychic symptoms. It is as important to interpret one as the other in determining the course of disease and the ultimate prognosis of the case. This is but a further evidence of the integrity of being and the efforts of the total being to work out its problems first in one way and then another. If aid can be furnished to the person working through his problems the quest for psychic escape from distress may be worked through so completely that the alternation comes to an end in wholeness of being and a higher level of integration in the personality.

The crises of life can be therapeutically useful. Ancient medical practice used various forms of shock, and the witch doctors still resort to it. In medical care of the psychotic a couple of generations ago the fall through a trap door into a vat of water with a bit of scattered hay on top was often a thirty-foot descent into health through a crisis. Electric shock and insulin shock therapies are refined uses of this method, as the name implies. The wise therapeutic intervention in catastrophic illness may expose the deeper problems of the individual, so that health is restored.

Terminal illness is often the dramatic end of a life conflict, but if the conflict can be resolved, the terminal nature of the illness may be changed. The reality of struggle in life is worked out in northern European religion, where forgiveness is rejected as an evidence of limitation on God's power. The element of conflict reflected in Nietzsche, who went back to Zoroaster (Zarathustra), is deeply rooted in life, and often becomes the basis for physical and emotional breakdown. Here again therapeutic intervention can resolve the problem and thus make the physical symptoms unnecessary.

The communication we speak of with the dying patient is hazardous, because it calls for a journey into the no-man's-land where no one can long claim omnipotence. There is an empty space, where the ultimate communion between man and God, creature and creator takes place. While it is a product of consciousness, it always implies more than mere consciousness. As lungs have no meaning without air, and eyes no meaning without light, so the capacity for God-consciousness raises the questions of ultimates, unknowns that cannot be treated lightly. We would all like to gain power over death by knowledge, by scientific achievement, by philosophic subtlety, but in truth all these efforts fall short when the unknown wind blows and none can tell whence it comes and whither it goes. We would like to capture the secret of life and the dying person often appears to be on the verge of capturing that secret. Sometimes we are afraid of the knowledge he may gain, and deny that it can exist for him, and at other times we hide our face, as if not to look into the too brilliant light. Man's ultimate challenge is in his death, whether it has meaning or whether it is the final triumph of meaninglessness. In pain, a person can endure much more if it has meaning to him. A prisoner in a German concentration camp said he was able to endure the beatings and the torture to which he could attribute some meaning, but when they stripped him, cut the buttons from his shirt, and sewed them on his skin, he collapsed with the pain, for the act was so completely meaningless. The quest for meaning gives to pain and death a direction and purpose. For the clergyman and the physician who honestly enter the quest, not with false claims of an impossible omnipotence but with the companionship of honest sharing, the very silence becomes rich in communication, for then they are sitting quietly together rather than quietly apart.

To believe, however, that it is within his duty, power, and providence to release the inner creative forces so that the patient does not die is extremely presumptuous on the part of the therapist. It is only natural when we are concerned and involved with a patient to want to do this. However, this impossible claim not only separates patient and therapist but also leaves the therapist with incapacitating feelings of guilt. To the Greeks, the gods themselves were subject to fate. The therapist, if he sets himself above fate, is false to himself and to the patient and greatly reduces his effectiveness.

The clergyman's presence may stand as a quiet symbol of the assurance that man's quest for eternal meaning still goes on. Without making unreasonable claims that cannot be substantiated, the symbol of faith can remain to the end an affirmation of man's quest for the finest of the inner kingdom where the "inside God" is to be found. Finding that, there is nothing further that is needed. This becomes the great illumination, that "I am," and this quest can be stimulated by anyone who stands close to the dying person, so that value is given to his living or dying.

The act of praying is the conscious effort to bring the encounter of the self and the beyond-self into active expression. This is an act that gives direction to the urge to do something. When the doctor says, "we have done all we can do, now we can only keep on praying," he is not giving a counsel of despair but is holding up the point of relationship where meaning and power can still be found. In fact, it has been this point of moving beyond a human agency to spiritual power that has often marked the turning point in illness. So it is wise to realize that no physician has the right to pass the sentence of death upon a patient, but rather to say: "From the point of view of our medical knowledge there appears to be no promise of hope that we can give, but we know there are more powers in this world than our minds dream of. Life is the great miracle, and we can keep on discovering life. The medical picture is only a part of the total picture. The rest may be hidden deep within you, for ultimately your faith is the source of your wholeness." The scientist with a limiting frame of reference projects a limited faith. What is needed is a larger view of man, a larger frame of reference for examining his nature, a larger faith for an enlarged life. When the Scripture speaks of the wages of sin being death, it may well mean that a limited view of life is sinful and that the larger view gives the faith that sustains life so adequately that death and dying become incidental to the larger meaning. When such a view is attained, science, medicine, philosophy, and religion may stand together in awe before the wonder, mystery, and power of life. This stance may well release a new understanding of the creative energy of being. To limit this creative energy is tragic; to set it free is to enhance the wonder of life itself.

164

The Scripture reminds us that except as we become as little children we cannot enter the inner kingdom. It may well be that the sense of unbounded wonder, so much a part of the little child, and so quickly destroyed in the processes of education and acculturation, needs to be restored as part of the preparation for the living that sets the limits to the act of dying.

In the face of death we must realize that none of us have any final answers as to its meaning. Those who claim such answers deceive themselves and those who turn to them. But we do have a common interest in the experience that all ultimately share. When we can face it with honesty, keep open the channels of real communication, surround it with loving concern of a real community that cares to the end, and enrich our understanding by an honest and unmasked dialogue among all concerned, the way may be open toward a new era in the care for the dying as well as our care for the living.

NOTES

Chapter I

1. Eissler, K. R. *The Psychiatrist and the Dying Patient*. New York: International Universities Press, 1955.
2. Butler, Robert N. "Intensive psychotherapy for the hospitalized aged," *Geriatrics*, Sept. 1960, 5:644-653; also an unpublished report, *The Life Review*.
3. Donne, John. *Devotions*, ed. by John Sparrow. Cambridge, England: Cambridge University Press, 1923, p. 92.
4. Bruno, Giordano. *On the Immeasurable and Countless Worlds*.
5. Edman, Irwin. "Giordano Bruno—A Soliloquy," in *Poems*. New York: Simon & Schuster, 1925, p. 12.
6. Pascal, Blaise. *The Thought of Blaise Pascal*. London: J. M. Dent, 1904, p. 85.
7. John 3:16; free translation from the Greek.
8. Alvarez, W. C. "Care of the dying," in *Journal of the American Medical Association*, 1952, 150:86-91.
9. Shakespeare, William. *Romeo and Juliet*, Act V, scene 3, ll. 88-90.
10. Zinsser, Hans. *As I Remember Him*. Boston: Little, Brown & Co., 1955.
11. Zinsser, Hans. *Spring, Summer, and Autumn*. New York: Alfred A. Knopf, 1942.
12. Frankl, Viktor. *From Death-Camp to Existentialism*. Boston: Beacon Press, 1959.
13. Caplan, Gerald. *Emotional Problems of Early Childhood*. New York: Basic Books, 1955.
14. Heidegger, Martin. *Being and Time*. Tr. by J. Macquarrie

and E. Robinson. London: Student Christian Movement Press, 1962.

15. Berdyaev, Nicolas. *The Destiny of Man.* New York: Harper & Row, Harper Torchbooks, 1960, pp. 249-265.
16. Tennyson, Alfred Lord. "In Memoriam."

Chapter II

1. Unamuno, Miguel de. *The Tragic Sense of Life.* Tr. by J. E. Crawford Flitch. New York: Dover Publications, 1954.
2. Hocking, William Ernest. *The Meaning of Immortality in Human Experience including Thoughts on Life and Death.* New York: Harper & Brothers, rev. ed. 1957.
3. Murals by José Clemente Orozco in the Baker Library, Hanover, New Hampshire.
4. Tolstoy, Leo. *The Death of Ivan Ilyich.* New York: A Signet Classic, 1960.
5. Shakespeare, William. *Part II of Henry VI,* Act III, scene 3, ll. 5-6.
6. Malinowski, Bronislaw. "The art of magic and the power of faith," in Talcott Parsons, ed., *Theories of Society.* New York: Free Press of Glencoe, 1961.
7. Weisman, A. D. and Hackett, T. P. "The treatment of the dying," in J. H. Masserman, ed., *Current Psychiatric Therapies.* New York: Grune and Stratton, 1962.
8. Weisman, A. D. and Hackett, T. P. "Predilection to death: Death and dying as a psychiatric problem," in *Psychosomatic Medicine,* 1961, 23:232-256.
9. Lindemann, Erich. "Symptomatology and management of acute grief," in *American Journal of Psychiatry,* 1944, 101:141-148.
10. Bowers, Margaretta, *Conflicts of the Clergy.* New York: Thomas Nelson & Sons, 1963.
11. Le Shan, Larry. "A basic psychological orientation apparently associated with neoplastic disease" in *Psychiatric Quarterly,* April 1961, 1-17.
12. May, Rollo. *The Meaning of Anxiety.* New York: Ronald Press, 1950.
13. Weisman and Hackett. "Predilection to death."

14. *Ibid.*
15. Meerloo, Joost A. M. *Patterns of Panic.* New York: International Universities Press, 1952.
16. Bromberg, W. and Schilder, P. "The attitudes of psychoneurotics toward death," in *Psychoanalytic Review,* 1936, 23:1-25.
17. Bryant, William Cullen. "Thanatopsis."
18. Weisman and Hackett. "Predilection to death."
19. *Ibid.*
20. Shneidman, E. S. and Farberow, N. L. *The Cry for Help.* New York: McGraw-Hill Book Co., 1961.
21. Menninger, Karl. *Man Against Himself.* New York: Harcourt, Brace & Co., 1956.
22. Dunbar, Flanders. *Emotions and Bodily Changes.* New York: Columbia University Press, 1954.
23. Weisman and Hackett. "The treatment of the dying."
24. Weisman and Hackett. "Predilection to death."

Chapter III

1. Bowers, Margaretta. *Conflicts of the Clergy.* New York: Thomas Nelson & Sons, 1962, p. 221.

Chapter IV

1. Weisman, A. D. and Hackett, T. P. "The Dying Patient." Paper presented at Forest Hospital, Des Plaines, Ill., Dec. 27, 1961.
2. Cappon, Daniel. "The dying," in *Psychiatric Quarterly,* 1959, 33:466-489.
3. Frankl, Viktor. *From Death-Camp to Existentialism.* Boston: Beacon Press, 1959.
4. Cannon, W. "Voodoo death," in *Psychosomatic Medicine,* 1957, 19:182.
5. Weisman and Hackett. *See* Bibliography.
6. LeShan. *See* Bibliography.
7. Beecher, Henry K. "Nonspecific forces surrounding disease and the treatment of disease," in *Journal of the American Medical Association,* 1962, 179:437-440.

8. Kierkegaard, S. "Sickness unto death," in *Fear and Trembling and the Sickness unto Death.* New York: Doubleday, 1954.

9. Maslow, Abraham H. *Toward the Psychology of Being.* New York: Van Nostrand, 1962.

10. *Ibid.*

11. Spinoza, Benedict. *Ethics.* Part 4, proposition 2.

12. Tillich, Paul. *The Dynamics of Faith.* New York: Harper & Brothers, 1957.

13. *Ibid.*

14. Moustakas, Clark E., ed. *The Self: Explorations in Personal Growth.* New York: Harper & Brothers, 1956.

15. Dostoevsky, Fyodor. *The Idiot.*

16. Fisher, G. M. "On the pseudo-humanistic education of the psychotherapist," in *Journal of Humanistic Psychology,* 1962, 2:19-22.

17. Montaigne, Michel de. *The Essays of Montaigne.* New York: Oxford University Press, 1941.

18. Jourard, Sidney M. "The rôle of spirit and 'inspiriting' and human wellness," in *Journal of Existential Psychiatry,* in press.

19. Federn, Paul. "The reality of the death instinct especially in melancholia," in *Psychoanalytic Review,* 1932, 19:429-451.

20. Freud, Sigmund. "On narcissism," in *Collected Papers.* Tr. by Alix and James Strachey. London: Hogarth Press, 1953.

21. Laurents, Arthur. *A Clearing in the Woods.* Unpublished.

22. Hesse, Hermann. *The Steppenwolf.* New York: Modern Library.

23. Maslow, Abraham H. *Op. cit.*

24. Rosenthal, Hattie R. "Psychotherapy for the dying," in *American Journal of Psychotherapy,* 1957, 11:626-633; reprinted in *Pastoral Psychology,* June 1963, 14:50-56.

25. Beecher, Henry K. *Op. cit.*

26. Jung, Carl G. *Modern Man in Search of a Soul.* Tr. by W. S. Dell and Cary F. Baynes. New York: Harcourt, Brace & Co., 1933.

27. Horney, Karen. *Neurosis and Human Growth.* New York: W. W. Norton & Co., 1950.

28. Maslow, Abraham H. *Op. cit.*

Chapter V

1. Holmes, Oliver Wendell. *Medical Essays*. Boston: Houghton Mifflin Co., 1891.
2. Eissler, K. R. *The Psychiatrist and the Dying Patient*. New York: International Universities Press, 1955.
3. Feifel, Herman. *The Meaning of Death*. New York: McGraw-Hill Book Co., 1959; *and see* Bibliography.
4. Weisman, A. D. and Hackett, T. P. "The treatment of the dying," in J. H. Masserman, ed., *Current Psychiatric Therapies*. New York: Grune and Stratton, 1962.
5. Meyer, Bernard C. "What patient, what truth?" in S. Standard and H. Nathan, eds. *Should the Patient Know the Truth?* New York: Springer Publishing Co., 1955.
6. Shakespeare, William. *The Tempest*, Act II, scene 1, 11. 141-143.
7. Weisman and Hackett. *Op. cit.*
8. Tolstoy, Leo. *The Death of Ivan Ilyich*. New York: A Signet Classic, 1960.
9. Wolff, Elsie S. "The magnificence of understanding," in S. Standard and H. Nathan, eds. *Should the Patient Know the Truth?* New York: Springer Publishing Co., 1955.
10. Frost, Robert. "Home Burial," in *Selected Poems*. New York: Henry Holt & Co., 1923.
11. Ethical and Religious Directives for Catholic Hospitals. St. Louis: The Catholic Hospital Association, 1949, p. 3.
12. Browning, Robert. "Ben Karshook's Wisdom" in *Poems*. New York: Nelson Classics.
13. Knight, James A. "Philosophic implications of terminal illness," in *North Carolina Medical Journal*, October 1961, Vol. 22, no. 10.
14. Benét, Stephen Vincent. "No Visitors," in *Selected Works*. New York: Henry Holt & Co., 1940.
15. Chicago Daily Tribune, Oct. 7, 1961.

Chapter VI

1. Ruesch, Jurgen and Bateson, Gregory. *Communication: The Social Matrix of Psychiatry*. New York: W. W. Norton & Co., 1957.

2. Ruesch, Jurgen and Kees, Weldon. *Nonverbal Communication*. Berkeley: University of California Press, 1956.
3. Ruesch, Jurgen. *Disturbed Communication*. New York: W. W. Norton & Co., 1957.
4. Ruesch, Jurgen. *Therapeutic Communication*. New York: W. W. Norton & Co., 1961.
5. Frank, Jerome, "The dynamics of the psychotherapeutic relationship," in *Psychiatry*, Feb. 1959, Vol. 22, No. 1.
6. Frank, Jerome, *et al. Persuasion and Healing*. Baltimore: Johns Hopkins Press, 1961.
7. *Ibid.*
8. *Ibid.*
9. Matthew 18:19; free translation from the Greek.
10. Rosenthal, David and Frank, Jerome. "Psychotherapy and the placebo effect," in *Psychological Bulletin,* July 1956.
11. *Ibid.*
12. *Ibid.*
13. Schmeidler, Gertrude R. and McConnell, R. A. *ESP and Personality Patterns*. New Haven: Yale University Press, 1958.
14. Frank, Jerome. *Persuasion and Healing.*
15. Adrian, Lord Edgar Douglas. *The Physical Basis of Mind.* London: Blackwell, 1951, pp. 7-10.
16. Hinkle, Lawrence E. and Wolff, Harold G. From the Study Program in Human Health and Ecology of Man, at New York Hospital and Cornell Medical Center.
17. Freud, Sigmund. *Collected Papers.* Tr. by Alix and James Strachey. London: Hogarth Press, 1953.
18. Menninger, Karl. *Man Against Himself.* New York: Harcourt, Brace & Co., 1956.
19. Dunbar, Flanders. *Emotions and Bodily Changes.* New York: Columbia University Press, 1954.
20. *Ibid.*
21. *Ibid.*
22. Heard, Gerald. *A Preface to Prayer.* New York: Harper & Brothers, 1944.
23. Thurman, Howard. *Meditations of the Heart.* New York: Harper & Brothers, 1953.

Chapter VII

1. Zilboorg, Gregory. Quoted in Oates, Wayne E., ed., *Christ and Selfhood*. New York: Association Press, 1961, p. 26.
2. Cassirer, Ernest.
3. Jung, Carl G. *Modern Man in Search of a Soul*. Tr. by W. S. Dell and C. F. Baynes. New York: Harcourt Brace & Co., 1933.
4. Frankl, Viktor. *The Doctor and the Soul*. New York: Alfred A. Knopf, Inc., 1955.
5. *Ibid.*
6. Nickson, James. Personal communication.
7. Luke 8:48; Matthew 18:14; free translation from the Greek.
8. Tillich, Paul. *The Courage to Be*. New Haven: Yale University Press, 1952.
9. John 1:12.

ANNOTATED BIBLIOGRAPHY

In recent years, hundreds of books have been published on death, dying, and related subjects. In the following selection, we have tried to cover most important aspects of the subject, using books that should be rewarding to those who want both a broad and an in-depth view of the subject.

Ariès, Philippe. *Western Attitudes Toward Death*. Baltimore: Johns Hopkins University Press, 1974.

    A beautifully written journey through the 2,000 years of Western culture examining the ways people have thought and felt about death from the perspectives of personal and social history.

Beaty, Nancy Lee. *The Craft of Dying*. New Haven: Yale University Press, 1970.

    From a literary perspective, the English tradition of *Ars Moriendi* is explored in order to understand what dying means to the person who seeks to live wisely and die well.

Bowlby, John. *Attachment*. New York: Basic Books, 1969.

    A profound study of the dynamics of human attachment throws light on the grief of dying persons and those about them by interpreting the ways by which emotion is developed.

Croissant, Kay, and Dees, Catherine. *Continuum: The Immortality Principle*. San Bernardino, Calif.: Franklin Press, 1978.

    The contents of this book first appeared as an exhibit in the California Museum of Science and Industry to show the scientific and philosophical evidence for the survival of physical death.

Douglas, Jack D. *The Social Meanings of Suicide*. Princeton: Princeton University Press, 1967.

This study attempts to bring Durkheim up to date with an emphasis on self-destructive behavior as significant behavior that tells much about our society, its values, and its impact on people who live in it and try to get out of it.

Durkheim, Emile. *Suicide*. Glencoe, Ill.: Free Press, 1951.

Originally written around the turn of the century and reprinted in this edition in 1951, this classic in the field of sociology was one of the first serious scientific studies of the problems relating to death and its impact on life, and, conversely, the impact of life that leads to death as escape.

Eissler, Kurt R. *The Psychiatrist and the Dying Patient*. New York: International Universities Press, 1955.

A psychiatrist dicusses psychological aspects, ideas, and theories about death with rich case material and treatment suggestions for patients who are dying.

Fairchild, Roy A. *Finding Hope Again*. San Francisco: Harper & Row, 1980.

A useful guide for professional persons called upon to guide people out of the depth of despondency and depression.

Feifel, Herman, et al. *The Meaning of Death*. New York: McGraw-Hill, 1955.

An imaginative collection of articles by prominent scholars in the field of death-studies ranging from the arts, religion, and philosophy to the sciences, physiology, and psychotherapy.

Feifel, Herman. *New Meanings of Death*. New York: McGraw-Hill, 1977.

Two decades after his *The Meaning of Death*, the author brings up to date the thinking on the subject of death to reveal changes in direction and new feelings about the scientific and cultural study of the final phase of life.

Flew, Anthony, ed. *Body, Mind and Death*. New York: Macmillan, 1971.

Excerpts from original writings from the time of the Greek philosophers to the present reflect changing attitudes and constant concerns in thinking about death.

174

Frank, Jerome. *Suggestion and Healing*. Baltimore: Johns Hopkins Press, 1961.

A study of the effect of nonmedical approaches to disease and the establishment of a constant for the placebo response as they have a bearing on the healing process.

Fulton, Robert. *Death and Indentity*. New York: Wiley, 1965.

A collection of articles relating to the identity crisis produced by death and dying, with extensive commentary by the author, a sociologist who is Director of the Center for Death Education and Research at the University of Minnesota.

Garvin, Richard, and Burger, Robert. *Where They Go to Die*. New York: Delacorte Press, 1968.

With control of infectious diseases and increasing longevity, the process of dying in nursing homes becomes a concern for humanity and social interrelationship.

Glaser, Barney, and Strauss, Anselm. *Awareness of Dying*. Chicago: Aldine Press, 1965.

A careful study of the death experience in hospitals, using a theory of awareness to examine the interaction of the patient and those who surround the patient.

Glaser, Barney, and Strauss, Anselm. *Time for Dying*. Chicago: Aldine Press, 1968.

The authors examine the movement of the patient through a time span that moves toward death and consider the hospital attitudes and structures of organized response.

Gorer, Goeffrey. *Death, Grief and Mourning*. New York: Arno, 1977.

An anthropological study that explores ideas and attitudes toward death in contemporary Britain and reveals the lack of social emotional support that produces unfortunate changes in life-styles and social patterns.

Grof, Stanislav, and Halifax, Joan. *The Human Encounter with Death*. New York: E. P. Dutton, 1977.

A psychiatrist and an anthropologist explore attitudes and methods of intervention that may significantly change the experience of dying in our culture.

Grollman, Earl. *Explaining Death to Children*. Boston: Beacon Press, 1967.

An anthology drawing from religion, psychology, sociology, anthropology, biology, and children's literature that seeks to help adults and children gain a more responsive attitude toward the seemingly inappropriate subject of death for children.

Group for the Advancement of Psychiatry. *Death and Dying: Attitudes of Patient and Doctor*. New York: Mental Health Materials Center, 1965.

In-depth studies of attitudes of persons in critical illness from the physician's point of view.

Gunther, John. *Death Be Not Proud*. New York: Harper & Row, 1950.

A famous author describes the death of his son and talks about the thoughts and feelings that go with the experience.

Henry, Andrew, and Short, James, Jr. *Suicide and Homicide*. Glencoe, Ill.: Free Press, 1964.

A study of aggressive behavior toward self and others seeks to explain the social and economic forces that are being acted out.

Hinton, John. *Dying*. Baltimore: Penguin Books, 1967.

An overview of medical, socio-medical, psychiatric, and psychological aspects of dying seen from the patient's point of view rather than that of the family and hosptial.

Hocking, William E. *The Meaning of Immortality in Human Experience*. New York: Harper & Row, 1957.

A well-known philosopher summarizes his thinking on life, death, human destiny, and the survival of the human spirit after the biological event of death.

Jackson, Edgar N. *Coping with the Crises in Your Life*. New York: Jason Aronson, 1980.

In this first basic text of the new discipline of crisis psychology, the author examines the emotional crises that develop in life both to understand them more fully and manage them more wisely.

Jackson, Edgar N. *Understanding Loneliness*. London: SCM Press, 1980.

In this book the author explores the impact, development,

and management of the feelings of isolation, abandonment, and separation, with recommendations for their wiser management.

Jacobson, Nils O. *Life without Death*. New York, Delacorte Press, 1971.

A Swedish physician takes a look at the phenomena of mysticism, parapsychology, and the survival issue to see what the impact of life is on death and the impact of death on life.

Kastenbaum, Robert, and Aisenberg, Ruth. *The Psychology of Death*. New York: Springer, 1972.

A broadly based treatment of most aspects of death — personally, socially, historically, and culturally — this book is basic to a library on the subject.

Kavanaugh, Robert. *Facing Death*. Baltimore: Penguin Books, 1974.

A Christian psychologist looks helpfully at the feelings related to the death experience from many perspectives.

Kübler-Ross, Elisabeth. *On Death and Dying*. New York: Macmillan, 1969.

Using a cohort of middle-aged cancer patients, the author explores the psychological processes observed in moving toward death.

Lepp, Ignace. *Death and Its Mysteries*. New York, Macmillan, 1968.

A priest-psychotherapist looks at the problems related to human mortality in relation to value systems and therapeutic perpectives.

LeShan, Lawrence. *You Can Fight for Your Life*. New York: Evans, 1977.

After nearly thirty years of research on spontanteous regression in cancer cases, the author summarizes his findings in seventy-one cases in which there appears to be a strong tie between the onset of the symptoms and a crisis of emotions. He finds that illness in such cases can be managed by modification of body chemistry through change in attitude and life-style.

Lynch, James J. *The Broken Heart*. New York: Basic Books, 1977.

Based on a ten-year study of patients in coronary care, intensive care, and trauma units, this book examines the medical consequences of isolation and loneliness.

Lyons, Catherine. *Organ Transplants: The Moral Issues*. Philadelphia, Westminster Press, 1970.

From the perspectives of medical science and Christian ethics, the author looks at the recent developments in surgery to assess their impact on our concepts of death and dying.

Neale, Robert E. *The Art of Dying*. New York: Harper & Row, 1973.

The author explores healthful attitudes toward death and the fears that often surround the dying process.

Pearson, Leonard, ed. *Death and Dying*. Cleveland: Western Reserve University Press, 1969.

Several significant papers on current issues related to the treatment of the dying person and those who emotionally and professionally interact.

Quint, Jeanne. *The Nurse and the Dying Patient*. New York: Macmillan, 1967.

Addressed primarily to nurses, this book speaks with special authority because of the author's research and personal experience as a nurse with catastrophically ill and dying patients.

Rahner, Karl. *On the Theology of Death*. New York: Herder and Herder, 1961.

The well-known Roman Catholic theologian writes of life and death as part of a process for achieving significant life within the philosophy and sacraments of the Church, which guards the passage from baptism to the last rites.

Schiff, Harriet S. *The Bereaved Parent*. New York: Crown Publishers, 1977.

A poignant and constructive look at the emotional stresses experienced by a parent at the death of a child.

Shneidman, Edwin S., ed. *Death: Current Perspectives*. Palo Alto, Calif.: Mayfield, 1976.

A collection of significant writings by many persons who have played a role in the emerging study of thanatology, revealing the many-faceted forms of interest in the subject.

Shneidman, Edwin S., ed. *Essays in Self-Destruction*. New York: Aronson, 1967.

A scholarly collection of essays with a focus on the literary, philosophical, social, and psychological dimensions of the subject.

Shneidman, Edwin S., et al. *The Psychology of Suicide*. New York: Aronson, 1970.

In an encyclopedic volume, the authors gather important statements on every aspect of suicide as basic reading on the subject.

Steinfels, Peter, and Veatch, Robert M., eds. *Death Inside Out*. New York: Harper Forum Books, 1975.

Scientists and physicians brought together by the Hastings Institute of Society, Ethics and the Life Sciences make a major contribution to the literature on death and dying.

Sudnow, David. *Passing On*. Englewood Cliffs, N.J.: Prentice-Hall, 1967.

A close-up view of the processes that surround the dying patient, from the moment the ambulance gives it special signals to the morgue and the way it is managed.

Troup, Stanley B., and Greene, William A., eds. *The Patient, Death and the Family*. New York: Scribner's, 1974.

Two physicians edit a book focused on the needs of a family that confronts the imminence of death.

Warner, Lloyd. *The Living and the Dead*. New Haven, Conn.: Yale University Press, 1959.

A sociologist explores the meaning and symbolism of a cemetery as it speaks constantly to those who travel in the land of the living.

Wesiman, Avery. *On Dying and Denying*. New York: Behavioral Publications, 1972.

A psychiatrist who has studied and counseled widely and wisely in this area of human concern sums up years of experience in an incisive and useful study.

Wolfenstein, Martha, and Kliman, Gilbert. *Children and the Death of a President*. New York: Doubleday/Anchor, 1966.

Observing the behavior of children in treatment for emotional disorders, the authors assess the impact of social violence on the therapeutic process.

179

Worden, J. William. *PDA—Personal Death Awareness*. Englewoo
Cliffs, N.J.: Prentice Hall, 1976.
An exploration of death anxiety and its gripping fear designe
to help set people free so that they may live more fully.